ST MARTIN'S
TRUE CRIME
CLASSICS

IT'S SHOCKING! IT'S BARBARIC!
IT'S HAPPENING TODAY!

- Alice spent years as a "maid," being beaten, raped, and physically and mentally tortured by her masters—members of an unimaginably rich Arab royal family.

- Stanya arrived to fill a position as a well-paid domestic, only to find that the agency that made the arrangements was really a front for a prostitution ring headed by a vicious, woman-beating pimp.

- At the palatial home of Rima's employers in Beverly Hills, the lady of the house ordered the chauffeur to flog the teenaged girl after every imagined affront.

- When Edita complained to the master of the household about the sexual attacks by his two sons, the man beat her fifteen times. She woke up to find him having sex with her on the floor.

YOU'LL NEVER FORGET THEIR HARROWING ESCAPES
AND TERRIFYING TRUE STORIES...

SLAVE GIRLS

WENSLEY CLARKSON

St. Martin's Paperbacks

SLAVE GIRLS

Copyright © 1996 by Wensley Clarkson.

Cover photograph by Alexa Garbarino.

ISBN: 0-312-95870-6
EAN: 80312-95870-1

Printed in the United States of America

St. Martin's Paperbacks edition / August 1996

St. Martin's Paperbacks are published by St. Martin's Press, 175 Fifth Avenue, New York, NY 10010.

15   14   13   12   11   10

AUTHOR'S NOTE

The stories of all these women are true. While all are based on actual cases, certain dialogue has been recreated and certain names and identifying characteristics of people depicted in this book have been changed, including Ana Gomez, Juliet Brown, Kathy Cannon, Cindy Wellington, Josephine Thompson, Betty O'Neil, Glynis Edmunds, Denise, Pam Sullivan, Stanley Pakula, Camilla Simmons-Ruiz, Lao, Ty, M. Nasaar, Muhammed Mahtoub, Meisa Mahtoub, Anila and Paula O'Neil. Otherwise, these women have been fully identified after speaking out on behalf of the tens of thousands of other slaves throughout today's world.

In telling these true stories it is not the intention of the author to demean any one class of people, but simply to reveal a life that seems a tragic indictment of our so-called civilized society.

To PMA . . . for all their endless encouragement.

NOTES OF GRATITUDE

The idea of using a leaden, dispassionate word like "acknowledgments" for this section cannot begin to express the depth of my feelings for the many individuals who have made this book possible. I owe them my deepest and most heartfelt gratitude.

First to my manager and literary agent Peter Miller, without whom this book would never have happened. His support and guidance have been very much appreciated. His team members, Jody, Harrison, and Uri, also deserve praise.

Numerous criminologists, journalists, policemen, social workers, concerned individuals, and most importantly, the families of the subjects themselves provided invaluable assistance—some from as far away as California and Japan.

A special note of thanks to Sgt. Tom Budds of the LA County Sheriff's Department, whose help was beyond the call of duty, considering his incredibly heavy workload.

Then there are John Glatt, Mark Sandelson, Martin Dunn, Nick Ferrari, Tewe Pannier, Simon Kinnersley, Joe Poalella, Sadie Mayne, Rosie Ries, Savage, Charlie Spicer, John Blake, Jon Ryan, Jon Wosnop, Pete Pickton, Viola, and Mir.

Also, my eternal thanks to the reference libraries at

NOTES OF GRATITUDE

News International, London and Chief Librarian Fagi at *The Daily News* library in New York, as well as to *The Sunday Times, Daily Telegraph, Daily Mirror, The Sun, The News of the World, Daily Star, Sunday Mirror Magazine, The Evening Standard, The Mail on Sunday, The New Yorker, The Los Angeles Times, Secret Magazine,* and *The Leather Journal.*

A special note of thanks to everyone at Kalayaan and Anti-Slavery International for providing details of certain cases as well as their superb booklet entitled ''Britain's Secret Slaves.'' Also Gordon Thomas's book *Enslaved* published by Bantam in 1990. And finally, to all other sources of reference material that have proved so inspirational for this book.

Slave n. **1.** a person legally owned by another and having no freedom of action or right to property. **2.** a person who is forced to work for another against his will. **3.** a person under the domination of another person or some habit or influence. **4.** a person who works in harsh conditions for low pay.

"I will cut your face. I will kill you and scatter your pieces in the desert if you ever disobey an order. You are my slave. You will do exactly what I say, eat only when I tell you and only what I give you. If you attempt to steal food, you will be starved until I decide you have learned your lesson. You will sleep on the floor outside my bedroom and only for the hours I tell you. You will have no days off and you will not leave this house unaccompanied. Remember, I hold your passport. If the police find you, you will be brought back to me. And if you are, you may be killed. Don't forget—there are plenty more where you came from."

The threat made to slave Alice Santos, just after she was "employed" as a domestic in the Middle East in 1992.

INTRODUCTION

Workers have been transferred in large numbers and over long distances since the end of the 15th century, from the enslavement of indigenous people to African slaves following the conquest of the Americas through to the present day.

However, although the world officially condemns slavery today, laws in many countries still consider domestic staff as household members and this non-recognition renders them liable to abuse. *It legitimizes slavery.*

In the Middle East, a region notorious for domestic abuse, even the conclusion of the Gulf War did not mark an end to the hostilities towards domestic servants. In 1994, it was estimated that thousands of women slaves were hiding in foreign embassies in Kuwait City following outrageous violence against them. Most could not leave the country because their passports were confiscated by their employers.

The status of women in certain Gulf states is thought to be a crucial factor. They have no right to vote and are still expected to be docile and subservient to their husbands. Some believe that female employers regularly punish their slave girls severely because they are treating their maids the way their husbands treat them.

As the cases in this book will sadly illustrate, it is indeed all too often women who are the most brutal employers when it comes to the abuse of female servants. Many experts believe this is because they are passing on elements of their own brutal treatment at the hands of their husbands.

Sexual and physical abuse is meted out by many nationalities: American, British, Indian, German, Nigerian, Spanish, and South African to name but a few. And it frequently takes place in the rich neighborhoods of some of the most sophisticated cities in the world.

One of the biggest problems is in London, where the wealthy in areas like Hampstead, Mayfair, Knightsbridge, Chelsea, and Kensington employ an estimated *five thousand* female domestic slaves. The women themselves come from all over the Third World, including Sri Lanka, India, Nigeria, Sierra Leone, North Africa, and some poorer European nations. However, the largest recorded number come from the Philippines via the Gulf states.

These domestic servants arrive in the United States, Britain, and other countries under special dispensations that allow employers to bring them in under one of two categories: as "visitors" or as "persons named to work with a specified employer." Immigration officials in Britain—where the slave issue has reached epidemic proportions—have even been issued highly confidential guidelines that allow any domestic who has been employed for at least twelve months to continue their employment in the United Kingdom. The guidelines clearly state that if domestics leave their original employer then they are deemed illegal immigrants in the eyes of the law.

In the United States, immigration rules that permit employers to bring domestic servants into the country, provided they continue working for them, have also opened the floodgates to abuse and slavery. Many of these women are abused behind the closed doors of so-called "respectable" homes.

Domestic servants arriving in countries like Britain and the United States naturally expect freedom to prevail at last. They presume they will be able to choose whatever job they want and walk away from the horrors inflicted on them by brutal employers. But none of them realize that a slave who has run away from an employer has no legal rights.

For the cruel truth about life as a domestic servant in many countries is that as soon as the work visa with a current employer expires, they automatically become illegal immigrants in the eyes of the law. In other words, if they run away from cruel employers, they will be automatically thrown out of the country. It is an archaic situation that encourages the continual abuse of domestics.

Employers of slave girls recognize this and frequently threaten their workers with dire consequences if they dare to escape.

In any case, fleeing is not easy: there are practical difficulties. Doors are kept bolted, windows locked and barred, and there may even be security guards or dogs patrolling the premises. Many women are simply not allowed out of the house, so they have no idea where they are, where to go, or how to get there. They have no money, no papers, no friends, no belongings. It is a leap into the unknown, and always there is the fear that their employers will discover what they are planning.

Recent moves by various governments to make employers set out in writing the main terms and conditions of work before allowing them to bring an employee into a country have done little to stem the influx of slave girls. What most employers promise in writing bears little resemblance to the way they intend to treat their servants.

Countries such as Great Britain, the United States, and the Gulf states all claim they are making further moves to curb the plight of the slave girls. Officials insist they are planning changes to the work permit rules that have been abused by the rich as a means to employ servants as slaves.

But these governments all say they can do little to prevent the abuse and humiliation of slave girls because most are terrified that if they report their employers they will themselves be deported.

Also, within many Western countries, there have been numerous cases of the slavery and imprisonment of women so they can be used as sexual toys, often with tragic results.

These women are beaten, starved and face nonstop

physical and sexual abuse. At night, many are chained to their beds to prevent escape.

It seems extraordinary that in these so-called modern times, the deliberate enslavement of women continues without any real interference.

Hearts live by being wounded.
　　Oscar Wilde

————

Suffering is permanent, obscure and dark/And
shares the nature of infinity.
　　William Wordsworth (1795)

————

SLAVE GIRLS

PROLOGUE

Think of a wealthy middle-class family and what do you see? A safe, comfortable home with a life of decency and attainable luxury. But in reality, some families have inflicted so much terror on innocent servants that it seems almost unbelievable in this day and age. The women in this book had no freedom, often no income, no control over their own lives, and no value but as an object to be physically and sexually abused. Hidden behind the veil of respectability, they became prisoners. Their jailers were often employers, their children, and other employees. Sometimes these women had been kidnapped off the streets and incarcerated.

Many were young, innocent girls sold to families for a few dollars. Some had not even reached their teens before being forced to leave their homes. Others were captured by sick and twisted people and forced into a nightmarish existence that in some cases cost them their lives.

It seems incredible, but many of these appalling

acts of violence and depravation were committed just a short distance from some of the most famous landmarks in the world, like London's Buckingham Palace, home to the Queen of England, the so-called savior to a nation that prides itself on freedom of expression and the right to choose. Others were enslaved in similarly civilized cities across the world. And it must be remembered that these women had no choice. Trapped inside often luxurious homes, they were too terrified to alert anyone to their plight.

Frequently, what should have been a golden opportunity to escape the repression and poverty of their homelands turned into a life filled with fear and loathing as they became the forgotten victims of apparently law-abiding people, who were proud to be part of a so-called civilized society, yet treated their servants like animals.

Slave girls remain hidden from the outside world in tiny cupboards or bedrooms, sometimes even bare floors on isolated hallways. They are treated like dirt and looked upon as human sponges expected to soak up abuse at the hands of their respectable masters and mistresses.

This book is a testimony to the indomitable spirit and great courage of these women, many of whom have spoken out for the first time, risking the full wrath of the people they have served in fear.

1

THE AMERICAN NIGHTMARE

Slavery is the status or condition of a person over whom any or all of the powers attaching to the right of ownership are exercised.
Article 1 (1) of the League of Nations
Convention on Slavery, Servitude, Forced
Labor and Similar Institutions and Practices
(1926)

NEW YORK CITY, APRIL, 1994

Her hair was thick, lustrous, and so dark it might have been spun on the same loom as the night. Her shoulders and back were slender. Her legs were just as perfect, except for the occasional bruise dotted along the inside of her thighs.

But then, petite Na had gotten used to pain since her arrival in the United States just twelve months earlier from Bangkok. During that period she had been forced to have sex with hundreds of men in a brothel/prison run by a gang of Chinese immigrants.

For Na, the American Dream had turned into a nightmare from which there seemed no escape. Every bone in her body ached. She had become numbed by the brutal sexual encounters and had rapidly concluded there was no goodness in the world, even beyond the four walls of that building in Manhattan where she had been incarcerated for so long.

Some days, she would suffer humiliating torture at the hands of brutal, uncaring clients who saw her as a sexual toy. On the good days, they would not beat her. It had gotten so bad that requests for straight sex were met with an overwhelming feeling of relief.

Na's nightmare began when she was halfheartedly helping out in her parents' grocery store in the Thai capital of Bangkok, daydreaming about a serious office job and a better life beyond the slums of one of the poorest cities in the world.

A local businessman walked into the store one day and made her a seemingly irresistible offer: He would arrange her passage to the United States and a job. It wouldn't cost anything because her future employer would pay her expenses.

A few days later, Na was greeted at JFK International Airport by two neatly dressed Chinese businessman in dark suits and immediately informed of the Faustian terms of her passage to the Big Apple. To pay off the people who had bought her ticket and arranged her visa, she was expected to work in a brothel and have sex with hundreds of men.

Na was terrified. The men pointed out that she had no choice. They had her return ticket and her passport. They even assured her that after she had sex with 300 men, her "debt" would be effectively repaid and she would be free to go.

Then they informed her of her new life: She would be held captive behind the locked doors of a Chinatown brothel where the "inmates" were known only by numbers instead of names, bars covered the windows, and buzzer-operated gates controlled the doors. She would not be allowed to leave the building until she had worked off that "debt."

Na began weeping in the Lincoln limousine as it whisked her towards her new, horrendous life. The two Chinese businessmen sat stone-faced and told her, "You have no choice."

Later she recalled, "I was stunned. I cried until they threatened to beat me if I did not shut up. I thought, 'I can't do anything. I am here. I can't do anything. I'm in their hands.'"

What Na did not realize was that she was just one of an estimated *two thousand* women held captive in the Chinatown district of New York alone.

When she was bundled out of the Lincoln and escorted into the dimly lit brothel/prison that would be her home for the next twelve months, she was shocked to discover thirty other women working in the cramped building under the enforced supervision of a madam called Siew Geok Adkins, better known to the girls and their clients as Lilly Chan or Jenny. A bouncer was on duty day and night to ensure that none of the girls tried to escape.

"You will stay downstairs until a man picks you

for sex, then you will take him to any of the spare rooms," Lilly Chan told the terrified Na within minutes of her arrival from the airport.

Just hours later the first of literally hundreds of men she would encounter came up the stairs from the sleazy street below. Na tried to hide her pretty face by holding her head down in shame, but Lilly Chan snapped at her, "Hold your head up, girl, or else I will tell them you are not working properly."

Dazed and jet-lagged from her long journey, Na could barely focus on the grinning figure who stood inspecting her and the other girls sitting around the lounge area of the brothel. She desperately tried to avert his gaze in the hope he would pick another girl. But she could feel his eyes burning down in her direction.

"You," said the man. "You. I want you."

Na did not move at first. Then one of the girls sitting next to her nudged her. "He wants you."

Na looked and tried to force a smile, fearful that she would be punished later if she did not respond. She got up and felt a cold shiver down her spine as the man grabbed her hand as if they were sweethearts rather two strangers.

Madam Lilly Chan led the couple up a rickety staircase towards a damp, dimly lit cubicle with a low-slung single bed over which a filthy towel was draped unceremoniously. She snapped the rates at the man and then shut the door behind them.

The noise of sex from the other cubicles wafted

across like a sick and twisted version of piped music in a restaurant.

Na tried to look away as the man undressed. She thought about her life at her parents' grocery store back in Bangkok and wondered why on earth she ever thought it was so boring.

"Bend over," said the man, snapping poor Na back to the awful reality of her situation.

Ten minutes later, she reappeared in the lounge area of the brothel with red eyes and a broken spirit. Her American Dream had just begun.

Life at 208 Bowery in the center of Chinatown went from bad to worse for poor Na and the other captive women at the brothel. The cubicles in which they were expected to have sex with clients were filthy and drafty. In each one, a cardboard box of the cheapest condoms lay unceremoniously on the floor.

Nearby, bouncer Joseph Morales—fat and sweaty—stood guard to ensure that none of the women tried to escape and their clients never got more than they paid for. Every night, Morales was allowed by Lilly Chan to pick one girl for a free bout of sex as part of his fee for working in the brothel. Na was one of his favorites.

Virtually all of the women working at the building had been lured by the same sort of promises as Na. And the "businessmen" who greeted her at the airport had a year earlier switched their attention to Thai girls after finding that their regular supply of Korean, Taiwanese, and Hong Kong prostitutes had dried up.

Customers at 208 Bowery paid a $30 admission fee and $100 for about an hour, although thankfully for the girls many of them were in and out within ten minutes. The women were expected to work from 11 A.M. to 4 A.M. every day of the week, and Na had sex with an average of two men per night.

For the first few weeks of Na's nightmare, she faced an angry backlash from customers and Lilly Chan because she was so sexually inexperienced. At one stage, Lilly Chan actually sat down the terrified young girl and told her how to satisfy a man. It made the girl sick to her stomach. Sometimes, Na was expected to go with two men at one time. She never received any payment. Instead, it went towards paying off her airfare and accommodations.

Little did Na realize that some of the girls working in the brothel had been bought outright by the evil Lilly Chan from the businessmen who provided them. She later admitted paying between $6,000 and $15,000 for many of the girls. One woman whom she bought for $9,000 had to pay her back in 270 "quotas"—270 men for $27,000. Other women—like Na—had to repay their smugglers by having sex with 380 to 500 men. All were charged $300 a week for room and board, payable through sex with three more men.

The prostitutes even kept track of how many men they had slept with in little booklets. Lilly Chan kept a master ledger so there were no later disputes over figures.

As the months passed, Na found herself unable to

fight back against the oppressive regime that now ruled her unhappy life. Her sexual encounters with complete strangers were becoming increasingly dangerous, as many of the men demanded certain sadistic practises.

Bruising was becoming commonplace. Sometimes they would bite her and then she would spend weeks fearful that she had caught AIDS or some other disease.

Her spirit was gone. Her determination to fight back had disappeared and she could see no light at the end of the tunnel.

Some of the other girls talked about escaping and going to the authorites, but most of them were convinced they would receive little or no sympathy. The girls considered themselves sordid hookers whom the outside world would rather not know about.

Madam Lilly Chan regularly told them they were worthless and that they would be lucky to be deported if detained by the immigration authorities. It was much more likely they would be arrested and sent to prison. Most of the girls believed her.

And any doubts that some of the stronger girls harbored were soon destroyed when Lilly Chan told them gleefully about how a girl who escaped from a nearby brothel had been murdered because she threatened to go to authorities.

It wasn't as if the police did not know what was going on at brothels such as the one on Bowery. But coerced prostitution of foreign women was especially difficult to combat because of its secrecy and the profit that drives it. In any case, it was virtually impossible to prove because the prostitutes often feared revenge and deportation and would not agree to testify against their masters.

Back at the brothel, Na and many of the other girls were suffering as badly as ever. Their only meal each day was a meager bowl of rice and some chicken soup if they were lucky. When one girl had been there about nine months, she was badly beaten by a client.

Lilly Chan would not allow the girl to be taken to the hospital for treatment, so a Chinese doctor was brought in. "But he was useless and we all ended up nursing her back to health," explained Na.

The attack on the girl made the other inmates of the brothel even more fearful for their own safety.

Eventually, city inspectors decided to try and close the building on the basis of housing code violations since they had long given up any hope of proving it was a brothel.

Checking the premises on October 11, 1994, they encountered two women—among 31 in the brothel at that time—who made it clear they wanted to leave.

That was enough of an excuse for the police to get involved once again, and it also brought interest from the immigration service. But authorities soon discovered that their efforts were fruitless because all the other women, including a terrified Na, were unwilling to speak out against Lilly Chan and the Chinese businessmen backing the brothel.

Then, on November 8, 1994, a prostitute managed to escape from the building and eventually called the other girls back at the house on Bowery, begging them to call the police for help "before it is too late."

In the police raid that followed, madam Lilly Chan was arrested, along with bouncer Joseph Morales and several others. Six more women turned themselves over to authorities; the rest were set free.

Since then, more than a dozen defendants—from brokers in women to their buyers—have been arrested, and slowly unfolded the inner workings of a modern international slave trade. Morales the bouncer was convicted of kidnapping and civil rights violations. Ironically, Lilly Chan turned state's witness at Morales's trial and told authorities cold-blooded details about how she oversaw the stable of sexual slaves.

As Russ Bergeron of the United States Immigration and Naturalization Service explained, "The network was very sophisticated. These women were provided with false documents, false ID's, and they were even rotated from city to city periodically in order to defeat law enforcement efforts."

Many officials believe that there are numerous such slave brothels throughout the United States feeding off people's desperation to gain entry into the richest country in the world.

"It's almost in the nature of what we have seen in alien smuggling, because of the high cost for people coming in," explained Daniel Molerio, the immigration agency's assistant district director for investigations, who helped supervise the raid on the Bowery brothel.

*   *   *

Luckily, Na's tale ends happily. After the immigration agency got working papers for her, she found a job at a Thai restaurant. One of her patrons fell in love with her and married her. She is planning to spend the rest of her life in America, where she hopes to raise a family.

2

FLOWER FROM THE HEAVENS

No one shall be held in slavery or servitude; slavery and the slave trade shall be prohibited in all their forms.
    Article 4 of the Universal Declaration of
    Human Rights (1948)

Rongmung Road, Bangkok, Thailand, Summer, 1989.

Frightened faces peer from the sordid shopfronts that have become rundown prisons for hundreds of young girls waiting to be sold into a life of enslavement. For Bangkok is probably the most notorious home to slavery in the world.

The street itself has an air of dread and danger. The innocent faces wait to be sold like items in a market. They will be raped and abused. Most will probably not live beyond the age of thirty.

Beady-eyed Western men prowl the street inspecting the available "goods." Many of them will buy a child to satisfy their sick lusts and perversions. Two weeks later, the same battered and bewildered girls will be dumped back on Rongmung Road where they will once again be forced to try and catch the attention of yet another master.

A cycle of poverty and desperation is mainly responsible for this appalling scenario. The child often becomes too expensive for her parents to maintain so she is passed on to a brothel or sweatshop where she can earn her keep.

Many of the girls are as young as 12 years old. Their impoverished parents sell them to shady figures like the sadistic Madam Paan Unkham. The parents receive no money from the evil brothel-keeper, just a promise that their daughters will eventually be sold to a Westerner who will give them the sort of life they could never expect on the backstreets of Bangkok.

The going price for a little girl is $200, but the amount of pretty young female sex slaves available on Rongmung Road means that many months could pass before someone buys them. Many will end up chained and abused by heartless sex fiends intent on finding ''fresh meat.''

Meanwhile, many of the slave girls are put to work in the brothels that service the hundreds of thousands of Western visitors to the sexual underbelly of the city, a place where intercourse with children as young as eight is openly available.

The so-called lucky ones are put to work in sweatshop factories where they receive virtually no wages except for a roof over their heads and a few scraps of food each day. Often, their parents get a small cash payment each month, but it is minimal.

One such slave girl for sale was 12-year-old Tatip Chanthon. Her beaming, innocent face soon attracted attention on the seedy Rongmung strip. She watched in horror as some of her friends were sold either to sexually depraved men or to so-called ''baby brothels'' that are dotted all over Bangkok.

Tatip emerged from the shadows into the burning heat of the noonday sun . . . a little girl lost, lonely and frightened. She was for sale to the highest bidder.

The little girl seemed resigned to her fate as a personal slave to a sweatshop owner, if she was lucky, or a sex pervert, if she was not.

By the end of the 1980s it was estimated that a staggering 800,000 girls under the age of 15 had been coerced into working as child prostitutes in the city.

Hundreds of the girls fall into the hands of pimps even before they reach the age of puberty, and one child welfare spokesman in the city claimed, ''I don't think Thailand has any virgins left over the age of 13.''

Not surprisingly, doctors believe the country's current AIDS epidemic has been caused mainly by the depraved behavior of uncaring men towards these innocent children.

Tatip had been sold by her parents and stood available for any sick and twisted perverts in one of the ten shop locations on a grubby side street just off the main drag and perilously near the city's main railway station.

But no one made an offer to buy her even though the dealers in flesh, who call themselves labor agents, confidently predicted to her parents that they would sell her "very quickly" and pass on a commission to her family.

As the days turned into weeks and there were no offers, Tatip was allowed to take a position further back in the shop, thus avoiding many of the evil eyes panning around for fresh, young meat to use and abuse.

The irony of the situation was that her family would never end up getting more than a mere pittance from the flesh dealers—and the children themselves often worked for nothing after being told that their wages were paid directly to their parents.

The open abuse of the system is clear for anyone to see, but little or nothing is ever done by the Thai authorities.

Tatip's "owner" was a woman called Kitiya. She did not care to whom she sold the young girl as long as they paid the $200 going rate.

"You can do what you like with her. She's a good girl. She will obey your commands," the heartless flesh dealer told one prospective buyer.

But Tatip was one of the lucky ones. She was bought by a British journalist writing an article on slavery for his newspaper. The little girl was immediately set free and sent back to a safe home where she would be treated well.

Reporter Peter Bond was even given a bogus receipt for Tatip. It claimed she was Thai while in fact she had been illegally smuggled over the border from Laos. Dealer Kitiya even declared a false address for the little girl and claimed she was 14. But then, no one ever checked the details. Tatip was just another slave girl; nobody would care.

Kitiya shamelessly took 5,500 baht ($200) for the girl, saying the sum included her first year's wages, and that there was no need to pay her another penny for the following twelve months.

Tatip's life would undoubtedly have been ruined if she had not escaped the clutches of this appalling woman.

Bond's newspaper, *The Daily Star,* in London, helped expose the evil trade in female child slaves, but sadly, their efforts have done little to reduce the alarming number of children for sale on Rongmung Road to this day.

The newspaper also exposed the primitive jungle trail that is used to transport children from across the Mekong River to Thailand, where they are sold as slaves on the streets of Bangkok.

The paper was appalled when offered little Tatip for $200. "She's 12 years old, and her name means Flower from the Heavens. She is yours," said the evil slave trader Madam Unkham when she was pitching the sale of the child to reporter Peter Bond.

Tatip was eventually sold to Bond with nothing more than the shabby clothes she wore and a bag containing a spare cheap cotton skirt. She was tired, hungry, and filthy . . . and she had been sold into slavery by her own parents. Tatip badly needed a bath and a new set of clothes after her gruelling three-day journey from her home deep in the Laos jungle.

When Bond later took her out for a meal, she admitted she had never seen such a spread of food, but could hardly eat a mouthful.

It then emerged that all she had ever eaten in her village were snakes, frogs, beetles, fish, and fried rice. She patiently explained why her parents sold her. "They have no money and with no rain it's difficult for them to find something to eat."

Tatip had heard strange rumors about other children in neighboring villages who had disappeared. But she couldn't believe that her parents would actually sell her off.

"I don't want to see them again after what they have done to me," she explained.

After being brought to the banks of the Mekong with six other girls, Tatip and her friends were handed over to the evil Madam Unkham, 41, who took the terrified children to be sold on the streets of Bangkok.

But before setting out on the journey, Unkham drummed into them what to say if questioned by a policeman or prospective buyer. They had to swear they came from a Thai village called Navang, where Unkham actually lived.

"None of us knew what was going to happen here, except that we were being sold," explained Tatip.

Tragically, this is an all too common occurrence in rural Thailand and Laos, where children are sold by their parents to pay debts when a crop fails or their rent increases.

Yet it is strictly against Thai law for children or adults to be brought into the country and sold for work. Cruel and heartless employers treat the young slave girls little better than dogs. They are beaten, starved of food, and paid a pittance, if at all.

Tatip had lived such an isolated life up until her trip to Thailand that she had absolutely no knowledge of the outside world. She had never heard of Europe or America, TV, pop music, or electricity. She had seen the odd car, but had never ridden in one before she got to Bangkok. At 12 years old, the youngster had never had ice cream or a single toy to play with. Occasionally, she'd seen airplanes but never wondered about them. She said, "They were just things in the air. They didn't mean anything, and they didn't harm us." Tatip only had two years of actual education, and mostly helped her father in the rice paddies near her home. He made less than $5 a month.

The little slave girl's home was a wooden house built on stilts. "We all lived and slept in one big room. I was happy there. But then my mother told me I would have to go away and work. She said she would get money for me. She told me I would have to work very hard for the man who took me to Bangkok."

Children like Tatip, trapped in Thailand's thousands of brothels and sweatshops, often persevere under appalling conditions because they are frightened of letting their families down. They also fear any money already paid out for them will have to be returned if they flee from a ruthless employer.

Tatip is now living with the family of child welfare expert Kamron Gunatilaka until her future is decided. Mr. Gunatilaka said, ''She will remain in our care and only go back to her family when she is old enough to make that decision for herself. No pressure will be put on her.''

Tatip was taught to read and write. She had little trouble learning as she was fairly bright. ''Hopefully then she can learn a trade and find her way in the world,'' added Mr Gunatilaka.

Soon after being rescued, Tatip even struck up a friendship with an eight-year-old Canadian girl who lived with her parents at Mr. Gunatilaka's house in Bangkok.

Officially, Tatip was classed as an illegal immigrant, but she was not to be returned to her parents since she told officials she did not want to go home.

POSTSCRIPT: Many other disturbing slave girl cases have emerged in Thailand in recent years.

Recently, more than 20 girls were rescued from a Bangkok sweatshop where they worked in strict silence from 6 A.M. to midnight—and were beaten mercilessly if they broke the rules.

In one backstreet, girls making mosquito nets were slashed across the head with heavy scissors for any minor infringement. Other young girls are known to have been burned, whipped, starved, chained up, raped, and kept in cupboards for days on end.

SLAVE GIRLS

In most sweatshops, young girls are forced to eat, sleep, and work in the same stuffy, overcrowded room.

Toiling 16 to 18 hours a day, seven days a week, is normal practice. And any slave girl who dares to spend more than three minutes in a stench-ridden toilet can expect a thorough beating.

Many of the sweatshops have windows and doors barred to prevent escape. Crooked policemen profit by accepting bribes and turning a blind eye.

For the desperate youngsters, suicide is often the only way out. As child welfare campaigner Kamron Gunatilaka explained, "Until there is concentrated and positive action, I'm afraid that more and more children will be sold into this terrible slavery."

In 1990, Thailand's government tried to take some action by backing new moves to clamp down on child slave racketeers. But even then the legal age for child workers was only raised to 13.

3

CELLAR OF HORROR

*Slavery they can have anywhere. It is a weed
that grows in every soil.*
  Edmund Burke, 1775

———

The house was plain and nondescript. For blocks
around in all directions, there was nothing but row
houses—street after street of grim, deteriorating
dwellings lying on their deathbeds with their chins in
the street. But Gary Heidnik's house was different. It
was not only set back a dozen yards from the sidewalk, but it was unattached on one side, leaving
enough space for a small yard and a driveway, which
led to the rarest structure of all, considering the neighborhood: a garage.

It was a ramshackle building made of badly weath-
ered board, topped with a row of barbed wire to keep
trespassers from climbing over from the alley. Heidnik had even lined the insides of the creaky doors

23

with metal after a group of neighborhood punks fired several shots at the building the previous summer. One of the bullets had damaged Heidnik's Cadillac and that had upset him very much because he was particularly proud of his cars. He even kept a 1971 Rolls-Royce, which he had bought for $17,000 the previous year.

Inside the house, Gary Heidnik had just brought prostitute Ana Gomez back to the property for sex—or so she thought. After ten minutes of inactivity in bed together, Heidnik started choking the girl until she almost passed out.

Then he handcuffed her hands behind her back and marched her down to the basement, where he forced her into a cold, damp, dimly lit room that smelled of mildew and dust. The chill air reminded Gomez that she was wearing nothing but a shirt at the time.

Heidnik then maneuvered her towards a lumpy, bare mattress that was pushed into one corner of the room. He picked up a small cardboard box and extracted from it a metal rod that had been bent in the middle to form a skinny *U*. Looking closely, Gomez saw that each end of the rod was threaded. Actually, the device was a commercially made product called a muffler clamp.

Heidnik ran one end of the clamp through a heavy chain, which he pulled from another box, and then forced the clamp over Gomez's ankle. A small metal bar fitted between the two prongs to seal off the open end of the U. He dug in the box again and came up with two nuts, which he screwed into the threads after first wetting them down with super glue. From out of nowhere, it seemed, he pulled a hair dryer and aimed that at the glue to make it dry faster. Then he repeated the procedure with a second clamp.

While Gomez lay there frozen in shock, Heidnik flipped the loose end of the chain over a five-inch-thick pipe that came out of the ceiling and ran across the room into the opposite wall.

Standing back to survey his handiwork, Heidnik nodded in satisfaction. "Sit down," he told her, pointing to the mattress.

When she did, he stretched out beside her, put his head in her naked lap and went to sleep.

Ana Gomez awoke the following morning to find herself still shackled and naked from the waist down. She was very cold. The floor and walls of the basement were bare concrete.

She refused Heidnik's offer of an egg sandwich and orange juice for breakfast, fearing he had poisoned it.

Then 43-year-old Heidnik began digging a hole in an exposed section of the floor. Gomez feared that he was making a grave for her, but he had other ideas on his mind. Heidnik told the girl that he felt it was time he had a wife and family.

"I actually want to get ten women and keep them here and get them all pregnant. Then, when they have babies, I want to raise those children here too. We'll be one big happy family."

Gomez shivered. He didn't have to tell her that she was Number One. Shortly afterwards he unzipped his pants and ordered her to take his penis in her mouth. After a few minutes he inserted it in her vagina and pumped away until he climaxed. Her enslavement had begun.

Later that day Gomez tried to escape and was hauled into a hole in the ground of the basement that Heidnik had been digging earlier. He dragged a piece of plywood over her and balanced several bags of dirt on top so she could not move. Gomez was bent double to such an extent that her chin was on her chest.

Heidnik returned a few minutes later with a radio that he tuned to a hard rock station. He left and didn't return for 27 hours. Gomez knew precisely how long it was because the station's deejays were fanatical about announcing the time.

Not long afterwards another girl called Juliet Brown was captured by Heidnik and shackled in the dingy cellar alongside Gomez.

Since the only article of clothing they were allowed to wear was a thin shirt, they often huddled together for warmth and pleaded for blankets and more clothing. Even worse was the lack of contact with the outside world, the constant sexual desires of their captor, and the ever-present threat of beatings if they disobeyed his orders.

Heidnik occasionally served them oatmeal for breakfast. But usually it was Pop-Tarts, crackers, and white bread. Dinner was rice and shriveled hot dogs. Sometimes he gave them fried chicken as a treat.

On the sexual front it became clear that Heidnik's primary aim was to get them both pregnant and each day he would demand sex from both of them.

He even tacked soundproofing material to the ceiling of the basement to muffle the noise they made during their regular beatings.

Soon after they were trapped in the cellar, Heidnik screwed a large eye hook into a ceiling beam about seven feet off the floor. If one of them misbehaved, he would put a handcuff on one wrist and the matching cuff through the eye hook. The woman being punished would have to stand for hours on end, with one arm above her head, unable to lie down, sit, or shift positions.

Shortly after this another girl called Kathy Cannon was captured by Heidnik and taken down to the cellar to join the other two women. Then came Cindy Wellington.

As the number of inmates grew, a pecking order developed. Gomez—the most streetwise of the group—was learning how to manipulate the manipulator. As time went on, she was punished less frequently than the others and worked herself steadily into Heidnik's trust.

One of Heidnik's favorite tactics was to pick one of the group to be in charge when he left them alone, a sort of officer-of-the-day approach. Later he would come back and ask the responsible one who had misbehaved so he could dole out punishment. Discipline usually consisted of being whacked with the shovel handle, but it also included a restricted diet, time in "the hole," or being handcuffed to the eye hook. If the one in charge said no one had misbehaved then Heidnik punished her.

Frequently he made them beat each other, and if the one administering the punishment was not doing it vigorously enough, he would reverse the roles. Or he would take over himself.

Heidnik's sexual appetite showed no sign of declining. It was a rare day when he didn't force at least one of them to have sex with him. Sometimes he would go from one to the other, like a bee pollinating a flower bed, until he finally climaxed or grew tired. Later he even forced the women to have sex with each other.

Hygiene was minimal. Heidnik had brought in a Porta-John for the women to use as a toilet, and for feminine hygiene he brought them tampons. But in the early days he refused to let them bathe. They had to clean themselves with disposable premoistened towels of the type many parents use on babies when changing their diapers. One day Cannon accidently pulled two of the towels out of the container, which sent Heidnik into a rage. Accusing her of wasting property, he laid into her with a shovel handle.

Later he relented and every day would take one of them upstairs to wash. They always carried their chains with them, even into the bathtub. After they soaked for a few minutes, Heidnik would push them onto the bed and have sex with them.

While the cleanliness situation improved somewhat, the food situation deteriorated.

One day he was feeding his two dogs—a huge part-

Labrador called Bear and a scruffy collie mutt named Flaky—when he had an idea: The next time one of the women needed to be punished, he grabbed a can of chicken-flavored dog food and ordered them all to eat. They balked. "Eat or take a beating," he commanded. They ate it. From then on dog food became a regular part of their diet. Later it would take on a much more grisly aspect.

By late January of 1987 a fifth girl was captured by Heidnik and shackled in the cellar alongside his other women. Josephine Thompson, a petite, soft-spoken 18-year-old had such small ankles that he had to use a pair of handcuffs on her legs.

Soon after this, Juliet Brown died after being hung from the eye hook by handcuffs. Her death presented a major problem for Heidnik. It not only set back his plan to gather a group of human baby machines, but he also had to figure out what to do with the body. If it were found, she could be identified. And if she were identified, she could be traced to him. Now and then, her sister or cousins still came by looking for her. He simply couldn't get rid of the body, he reasoned; he had to destroy it.

Hoisting Brown over his shoulder like a sack of cement, Heidnik carried her up the steps. Sometime later the women in the basement heard what they thought was a power saw. They looked at each other and shivered.

Heidnik's dogs Flaky and Bear appeared several hours after he had taken Brown's corpse out with a

29

long white bone with chunks of red meat clinging to it. The women looked at the bone, and each thought the same thing: I wish I were close enough to grab the meat.

A few days after Brown died, Heidnik bought a food processor and used it to grind up parts of her body. He even mixed the processed meat with dog food and fed it to his dogs and surviving captives. The rest of her body was put in white plastic bags and stacked neatly in the freezer compartment of his upstairs refrigerator.

The parts he could not grind—the head, hands, feet and rib cage—he tried to destroy by cooking. That created a terrible stench, though, which almost choked the women in the basement and was so pervasive it was noticed by many of Heidnik's neighbors.

Eventually some residents alerted the police. But a rookie cop encountered Heidnik, who convinced the officer he had simply overcooked his dinner, and no other action was taken. The smell hung around for days, polluting the air, permeating what little clothing the women captives had, and, most noticeably, virtually soaking into Heidnik himself. That night—for the first time since he took his first slave on November 26—he did not go down to the cellar for sex. But for many days afterwards, when he resumed his sex-fix visits, he smelled so strongly of burning flesh it was all the women could do to keep from gagging.

Heidnik didn't know it yet, but his days were numbered; his grandiose plans for creating a basement baby factory were rapidly unraveling. Before they collapsed completely, however, his captives would undergo more suffering and another would die.

Between February and March, 1987, Heidnik carried out a number of horrendous punishments on his sex slave girls. These included:

Hanging each of the girls, one by one, to the eye hook, cuffing them with one hand above their heads and both their ankles. Then he would stuff a plastic bag in their mouths as a gag and secure it with duct tape wound around their heads. Finally, lopping an arm around their throats to hold them still, he took a screwdriver and gouged in their ears, trying to damage their eardrums.

"He used three kinds of screwdrivers," said Cannon later. "Small, medium, and large. He twisted them in our ears until pus came out."

Showing any badly behaved slave Juliet Brown's head in a pot as well as her ribs in a roasting pan and a bunch of her other body parts in the freezer.

Snipping off the plug end of an ordinary electrical extension cord and stripping the insulation to leave a bare wire. Then he plugged the other end into a socket. With current then flowing through the wire, he touched the bare end to the women's chains and laughed while they jumped and screamed.

*　　*　　*

Shortly after this, Cindy Wellington died when three of the girls were crammed in the hole in the cellar and Heidnik began electrocuting them. The wire went straight to her chain and so she took the heaviest jolt and died instantly.

At first Heidnik refused to believe that she had died. However, eventually he dragged her corpse out of the hole and laid it down in a far corner of the cellar.

"Aren't you glad it wasn't one of you," Heidnik commented casually before calmly starting to make dogfood sandwiches for his slave girls.

Shortly after this, Heidnik began to give Ana Gomez considerably more freedom than his other slaves. He continued to have oral and vaginal sex with each of them with the intention of getting all or some of them pregnant.

Eventually, Gomez managed to make her escape by convincing Heidnik that she would go out and get him a replacement for the recently departed Cindy Wellington. Instead she went straight to the police.

Just before midnight on March 24, 1987, police detained Heidnik outside his house and took him in for questioning. He insisted he had done nothing wrong.

The following morning at 5 A.M. police armed with a search warrant crowbarred the front door of the house after failing to open the door with keys provided by Heidnik. Once the door was knocked down, the police headed for the cellar.

All around the room were white plastic shopping bags. A mattress was lying in the middle of the room and on it were Kathy Cannon and Josephine Thompson, covered in blankets and snuggled up against each other for warmth. They were asleep.

When they heard the commotion, they jerked awake and started screaming.

The women bolted to their feet, letting their blankets drop. Except for socks, they were both nude from the waist down. Both had shackles on their ankles that were connected to heavy chains.

"Are there any other women in the house?" asked one of the cops. "Is there anyone here but you?"

Both pointed to a pile of white plastic bags sitting on a board on the other side of the room.

"She's there," said Cannon.

One of the cops remembered Gomez's early claims about dismemberment and picked up one of the plastic bags.

"Here?" he asked incredulously.

"No, under the board," Cannon replied. "She's in the hole."

The cop pushed away the bags and slid the board aside. Squatting at the bottom of a shallow pit was another woman called Betty O'Neil who had been recently captured by Heidnik. She tried to stand up, lost her balance and tottered. The cops grabbed her arm and lifted her out. She was completely nude and shackled like the others and her hands were cuffed behind her back.

"We're free," cried Cannon and Thompson. They

grabbed the two cops' hands and smothered them with kisses. "We're saved!" they shrieked.

One of the cops dug out a handcuff key and tried to unlock the bracelets binding O'Neil's hands. It didn't fit.

The other officer offered his cuff key and it did the trick. Then they got on and removed her leg irons.

The women's ankles were covered with bruises and sores. Some were fresh, but many had scabs. The police couldn't undo the nuts and sent word upstairs to fetch some bolt cutters. They also called for an ambulance and some extra hospital overalls for the women to wear.

The slave girls were skinny and looked like POWs. They were also starving.

"He kept ice cream in the freezer," said Thompson, pointing to the same box where Cindy Wellington's body had been kept until Heidnik found a place to dump it. "Can we eat that?"

"I don't think you ought to have anything quite yet," said one of the cops. "Wait until the doctors check you over."

When their ankles had been freed they were taken through the dining room where Heidnik had left some cookies on the table. They grabbed them and wolfed them down.

As the women were whisked off to the hospital, the police fanned out through the house and began a painstaking search of the premises. On the shelf in a closet they found a large stack of porno magazines, all of them featuring black women.

While one cop went upstairs, his colleague went into the kitchen. He looked at the stove and noted an aluminium pot. The inside was scorched and covered with a yellowish material. In the open oven he saw a metal roasting pan that was charred on the inside and contained a piece of bone that looked suspiciously like a human rib. On the counter was a heavy-duty food processor, obviously used. The officer opened the freezer and, right there on the front shelf, was a human forearm.

That was too much even for the hardened, 20-year veteran. Feeling the bile rise in his throat, he ran outside and gulped the fresh air, trying mightily to keep from vomiting.

On July 2, 1988, just one hour and fifty-five minutes after they had begun deliberations, the jury at the trial of Gary Heidnik pronounced the death sentence for each of the murders of Juliet Brown and Cindy Wellington.

Heidnik showed no emotion, but one of Brown's sisters sobbed quietly in the public gallery.

The killer's lawyer asked the judge to make sure Heidnik was kept in isolation at prison in case other inmates decided on some rough justice. The judge refused.

Outside the court the sister of Heidnik's murdered slave girl Cindy Wellington told reporters, "My sister can rest in peace. We got what we wanted."

On his way to prison in Pittsburgh, guards stopped the bus to transfer other inmates and Heidnik was left alone momentarily with other prisoners. As soon as the guards' backs were turned, they jumped him, and were still beating him when the guards rushed back to break it up. Such an incident, in prison slang, is called "a tuning up."

But it was nothing compared with being put in a hole in the ground. No one beat him with shovel handles. No one dug his ears with screwdrivers. And no one plugged him in to see if he shone like a floodlight. It is ironic that the punishment he is eventually due to receive actually fits the crime he committed. For he is scheduled to be electrocuted—the same way his second victim, Cindy Wellington, died.

4

FEAR AND LOATHING IN SHIMODATE

Servitude debases men to the point where they end up liking it.
Vauvenargues, *Reflections and Maxims* (1746)

The town consists mainly of a soulless grid of convenience stores and amusement parlors stuck on the outer reaches of the Tokyo commuter belt. Its residents are made up of prosperous farmers, bored bureaucrats, and corporate workers.

But beneath this dull veneer, prostitution thrives. Bars and ''love hotels'' run by Japanese gangsters, the Yakuza, clog the backstreets, their neon signs flickering garishly. In dark alleyways, scantily clad women try to beckon men for sex. On the main street, drunks wander from club to club.

Just a few months earlier, Goong, Roon, and Noi—all in their mid-twenties—were living in Thailand's rural north. Goong, a lively, oval-faced woman, was supporting her elderly parents on a meager hospital cleaner's salary.

Roon, a svelte divorcée with a seven-year-old daughter, was juggling three part-time jobs. Noi, a frail 25-year-old, was working 12-hour shifts in a local sweatshop. None could resist when they were approached by friendly recruiters offering big wages as waitresses or factory workers in Japan.

Goong was the first to realize she had been horribly duped. On arrival in Shimodate, she was met by a broker who promptly "sold" her for two million yen ($20,000) to a woman called Lek, a 28-year-old Thai with cropped hair and sullen features who ran a prostitution racket in league with the Yakuza. Roon and Noi later met the same fate.

Within hours of their landing in Japan, Lek told the three women how the system worked: they now owed her 3.5 million yen ($33,000) each to cover their purchase price and her own profit, and they would have to sell their bodies to pay her back.

Lek took their passports, cash, and return air tickets. "If you escape, I'll turn the world upside down to find you," she warned. "If I find you, I'll kill you. If I don't, I'll send someone to kill your parents."

Goong, Roon, and Noi were then taken to Lek's apartment in Shimodate. They were terrified, bewildered, and very homesick but they had no choice.

Within hours, Lek had introduced them to other

Thai slave girls whom she "owned," and they were told to start work in a local bar called the Mimi. Their jobs were to pour drinks and clap girlishly at customers' karaoke efforts. But their real duties were soon made clear: to provide sex for men looking for relief from the tedium of their lives in the Tokyo suburbs.

The three women were stunned. None of them had ever done such "work" before. "Prostitution was against everything I believed in," Goong later recalled. "I couldn't accept it. My misery was too painful to describe."

Lek had an arrangement with the Mimi bar whereby the Thai women would work on the premises for nothing, and in return the bar would be a front for her shameless pimping.

Goong, Roon, and Noi were expected to have sex with at least three men every night and they were not allowed any time off, even when they were sick.

Goong later explained, "The customers often liked to do things they would never do with their wives." That included regular demands for fellatio, which all three of the women particularly hated.

One time, Goong refused to have oral sex with a man because of his lack of hygiene. When he complained to Lek, she dragged Goong from the room where they were having sex in her apartment and beat her. Goong was later convinced that Lek got a sexual kick from hitting her.

Lek later further punished Goong by telling all prospective clients that the girl gave "excellent blow jobs."

And the other girls did not fare any better. Noi was almost drowned by a customer after she refused to let him perform anal sex on her. He dunked her head repeatedly in a hot bathtub and then forced her on her knees.

All three slave girls were regularly spat on, punched, and burned with cigarettes. And some clients insisted on using handcuffs and other manacles during sex. "The men treated us like animals," explained Roon.

A police station stood just 300 yards from the apartment block where Lek was running her brutal regime. However, the women could not go there for help because many of the local police were customers, and Yoko Sasaki, the tough woman owner of the Mimi bar, warned them that a simple payoff to the police by the Yakuza would ensure that any allegations would be reported directly back to Lek.

"In any case, the police would arrest you for being illegal immigrants," warned Lek. The isolation of the slave girls was complete.

They spoke no Japanese and were never allowed out alone. They could write to their families, but Lek censored all the letters. She also pocketed every yen of the women's salary to repay their "debt," and devised a strict system of fines to ensure that their tab never reached zero.

The cost of everything, from their food to their frayed secondhand dresses, was billed to them. If three days passed without a customer they were fined $230. Lek said men preferred skinny girls and allowed them to eat only two meals a day. They often felt dizzy with hunger.

As the months slowly passed, the three slave girls began to doubt that they would ever escape alive. Lek issued daily death threats, boasting that she knew their addresses in Thailand and had the right connections to keep her word.

"Even if we had paid off our debts, she would never have released us alive," says Roon today. "We knew too much about her." In sheer desperation, Goong, Roon, and Noi slowly decided they had no choice: they would have to strike first.

At 5 A.M. on a crisp autumn day in September, 1991, Roon was awakened by Goong pulling at her arm. "I can't stand it anymore," she whispered. "We have to do it now."

Roon crawled out of bed well aware that only Lek and her two slave girl companions were in the apartment that night. Goong went to fetch Noi. The three talked in whispers until they all agreed that Lek had to be killed.

They headed for the kitchen where the only potential weapons were a small knife, a bottle of sake, and a garden trowel. Goong handed the knife to Roon in silence. Roon's hands shook so much that she gave it back. For a few endless seconds, the three passed the knife between them until Noi, the youngest and seemingly most faint-hearted, finally accepted it.

As dawn broke, the three women crept to Lek's bedside. She was sleeping curled up on her side, making a clean hit difficult. Goong put her hands together and prayed: "If Lek's life is to end tonight, please, God, let her turn over."

To Goong's amazement, Lek instantly complied. Neither Roon, Goong, nor Noi can recall who actually struck first.

"I saw Noi raise the knife and I closed my eyes," recalls Roon. "Lek screamed. Then I heard the sound of a bottle shattering and the smell of sake filled the room."

Lek began to thrash wildly. Goong shouted for Roon to hold the wounded woman's legs to stop them from moving. There was blood and broken glass everywhere.

A few minutes later, Lek fell still—unconscious or dead, the slave girls didn't know. Goong told Roon to help her remove Lek's gold jewelry, while Noi searched for the waist pouch where they thought Lek kept their passports. Noi grabbed Lek's locked red handbag in case their documents were in there.

The three women then made off across the rice paddy in front of the apartment complex. At the other side, they hailed a taxi and gestured for the driver to take them to a hotel. Once inside their room, Goong washed the bloody jewelry. This was to be their air tickets home, together with 200,000 yen ($2,000) in bar tips that they had saved by sewing the money into their dresses.

Roon forced open Lek's handbag to see if their passports were inside, while Noi unzipped the waist pouch. When the contents of both bags tumbled out, the three were stupefied. The hangbag contained a mountain of gold jewelry, the pouch nearly seven million yen ($65,000).

Back at Lek's place, one of her other slave girls discovered her corpse and called the police. By the time investigators arrived, Yoko Sasaki and her Yakuza gangster husband were there to enlighten police about what might have happened. They claimed the three women were "cold-hearted whores" who had a grudge against Lek.

Detectives soon tracked down the three runaway slave girls at their hotel by using the taxi driver's logbook. They immediately confessed to the killing but insisted they only thought about taking the money after Lek had been stabbed.

"We only wanted to escape," said Roon. But the police were highly suspicious. To add to the confusion, none of the women spoke Japanese so two Thai housewives had to be recruited to act as interpreters.

Nine hours later, the slave girls were presented with statements written in Japanese and asked to sign them. "I thought I would get home sooner if we signed," said Noi later.

At this stage the women were not even using lawyers. Three weeks after the stabbing, Goong, Roon, and Noi were charged with murder in the course of a robbery. The authorities cited their "signed confessions" as justification for the charge.

The case whipped up a lot of controversy in Japan because it was the first time that victims of the flesh trade had actually killed to escape. Young female lawyer Chinami Kajo took on the case and immediately insisted, "It was clear that the women's circumstances had been completely ignored by the police. They didn't want to admit that the problem of sex trafficking was involved because then they'd have to take action against the pimps and brothel owners. Most police don't want to get their hands dirty fighting prostitution rackets."

Kajo and her team of five lawyers decided to fight for a complete acquittal on the grounds of self-defense.

The odds against them were astronomical. In Japan's non-jury legal system, a staggering 99.4 percent of criminal cases are won outright by the prosecution, mostly on the basis of signed confessions. "The confession is the highest form of evidence here," explains one Japanese legal expert. "When the prosecution bases its case in such evidence, the judges rarely dispute it."

When the slave girls' trial began in December, 1991, the lawyers' first task was to try and discredit Goong, Roon, and Noi's supposed confessions. They claimed that untrained interpreters had been unable to translate the difference between "murder and theft" and "murder in the course of robbery," so the women had no idea what they were confessing to.

Another uphill task was for the defense to prove that Goong, Roon, and Noi had been forced into a life of sexual slavery. "We had to show they had fallen prey to international flesh traders," explains Kojo. "But we had no witnesses—it was impossible to find recruiters and brokers responsible.''

Even more surprising was that even if they had found the perpetrators, it would have been virtually impossible to prosecute them because of Japan's draconian attitude towards slavery.

There are no laws relating to the trafficking of women into Japan, only a nineteenth-century statute that prohibits the sale of Japanese women abroad.

The defense team did have one woman—bar owner Yoko Sasaki—to accuse of flagrantly abetting prostitution. But she wasn't too worried because she had landed the plum role of star prosecution witness. Sasaki insisted that she played no role in the prostitution racket.

Victim Lek was herself proving to be a real mystery. After her death it took the police 61 days to identify her. She had first come to Japan in 1983 and had been deported once, probably as a result of the same prostitution activities she had since forced on others.

All that was left of her was a ledger in which she had logged her employees' debts and her human purchases. Between 15 January 1990 and her death, she had bought 28 women for 56 million yen ($500,000).

Kajo and her team resorted to using experts who could testify about the sex slave trafficking industry between Thailand and Japan. One of them, Buddhist temple chief priest Akimichi Sugiura, told the court, ''Recruiters in Thailand target rural areas to find naive women. They are the first link in the chain, and are often local people or, most insidious of all, women

who were once victims of forced prostitution themselves. They pass on their female prey to members of
organized crime syndicates.''

Sugiura believes the flesh trade between Japan and
Thailand is worth up to $900 million a year. Most of
the women are brought to non-urban areas of Japan
where demand is highest and law enforcement less
rigid.

In Ibaraki alone—the region that the town of Shimodate belongs to—there are some 4,000 Thai female
sex slaves working in up to 400 prostitution bars.

Throughout Japan, there are believed to be 90,000
such women from Thailand and other southeast Asian
countries such as the Philippines and Malaysia.

Although it was impossible to prove whether Lek
would ever have carried out her threat to murder
Goong, Roon, and Noi, their defense lawyers argued
their fears were not unfounded. For a total of 43
southeast Asian women have died in prostitution-
related killings in Japan since 1991. And at the very
same time as the Shimodate trial, a Thai pimp was
prosecuted in a nearby city for hiring a hitman to
murder two prostitute slave girls who'd escaped without paying off their debts. The hitman had already
been convicted.

But at the trial of Goong, Roon, and Noi, prosecutors continued to insist that claims the three slaves
had acted in self-defense were completely bogus.

Sasaki told the court that Lek behaved like a
mother towards the three women. She actually

claimed the slave girls only ever worked as bar hostesses and never as prostitutes.

In his closing argument, the prosecutor proposed that Goong, Roon, and Noi be sentenced to life imprisonment, as a deterrent to "similar crimes by foreigners." He did not ask for the death penalty, but the news was still a blow.

At the final hearing in March, 1995, the three women pleaded for understanding. "I'm truly sorry we killed," said Goong. "I am quietly seeking forgiveness every day."

Roon promised never to commit such a crime again. "I have decided to become a nun when I return to Thailand," she told the court.

A distraught Noi could only croak, "I'm sorry."

On the day of the verdict, May 23, 1995, supporters of the three women were camped outside the provincial courthouse in force. Sympathy for their plight had gathered momentum, particularly because two virtually identical killings occured almost a year after the Shimodate murder.

Six Thai women killed a Taiwanese brothel keeper in Tokyo during an escape attempt; later that year five Thai women stabbed their Singaporean boss to death outside the capital. The fact that there was no robbery involved in either of those other cases raised the possibility in a few minds that maybe Goong, Roon, and Noi had been telling the truth.

The three runaway sex slaves could barely muster shy smiles as they were led into the tiny courtroom to hear their fate. They were dressed in jeans, white

T-shirts, and plastic prison slippers. They stood facing the three judges as the verdict was read out: they were declared guilty of murder in the course of robbery and sentenced to ten years imprisonment each. Goong and Noi began to cry. Roon remained expressionless.

The judge then explained the verdict. A call for life sentences had been rejected because, significantly, the women were deemed to have been under "mental and physical strain." But the claims of self-defense were also disregarded. The women, he said, had conspired to rob Lek and killed her in a "brutal manner." Kajo immediately announced plans to appeal.

The three women were inconsolable. "All the energy we've put into trying to explain the truth has been wasted," said Goong. "How come they still don't believe us?" Noi too was "shocked and upset."

Roon had other things on her mind. "When will I see my daughter?" she pondered miserably.

Strangely, however, the trial had some positive results. By showing the terrible extremes to which Goong, Roon, and Noi had been driven, it shocked more people into joining the fight against sex trafficking and slavery. "Now more groups and individuals realize that such slavery still exists here and must be stopped," says lawyer Chinami Kajo. She points to the need for stricter laws against the flesh trade, and to shift the current focus of punishment from the prostitutes to the pimps. "There is no excuse for police inaction now."

Goong, Roon and Noi are also aware that their case is a cautionary tale. "We want to publicize our experience as much as possible,'' says Goong from prison, ''to prevent other women from falling into the same trap.''

But the women still have a long, hard fight against a judgement that has branded them as callous, calculating killers. Their appeal could take two or three years and, if unsuccessful, that time will not be deducted from their sentence. They have no idea when they will see their families again.

''My life is adrift in the middle of the sea,'' wrote Goong shortly after her initial arrest. More than four years later, the women know they are still a long way from shore.

5

A TWISTED MIND

The moment the slave resolves that he will no longer be a slave, his fetters fall. He frees himself and shows the way for others. Freedom and slavery are mental states.
Mohandas Karamchand Gandhi (1949)

Susana's face had an affinity for light. Her skin was pale chocolate. Her dark hair still glistened despite the dreadful conditions she lived in. But it was the brown of her eyes, like jewels on velvet under a storekeeper's spotlight, that were her most defiant feature.

Even during the most terrible of physical attacks, those eyes refused to yield to fear. They beamed strongly, never giving away any of the terror that she must have felt when she was suffering from yet another beating.

Jorge Ferreira looked into them and was infuriated

51

by their warmth. For within his blubbery exterior lay a twisted mind. A mind warped by time. A mind that wanted her all to himself. A mind determined to get what he required—whenever he felt like it. How dearly the innocent Susana would have to pay.

"I'm so hungry, señor. Please, there must be something to eat." As she looked up at him, her chains rustled. Ferreira looked down at her with disgust and contempt.

"Shut up, nigger."

"But please, señor. Anything."

A smirk crossed Ferreira's face.

"Anything?"

"Yes. Please . . ."

He picked up a lump of cow dung from the floor of the barn and squeezed it in his huge hand.

"Try this, nigger."

Moments later, poor Susana was gagging as Ferreira tried to ram the stinking cow dung down her throat. He pinched her nose and forced some of it into her mouth.

"Never ask me for food again."

Ferreira gave her a kick in the kidneys for good measure and marched out of the secluded barn that stood 300 yards from his vast mansion in the remote village of Sao Joao de Loure, 160 miles north of the Portugese capital of Lisbon.

Another day in the tortured life of slave Susana dos Santos had come to an end. The few hours of sleep she got every night in that drafty outhouse were a welcome relief from the harsh reality of her situation.

*   *   *

Susana and her friend Emilia's suffering began 16 years earlier in the Angolan jungle, where Ferreira had settled during the fifties. At the time, Angola was a colony, and the Portuguese were very much in control.

Ferreira actually made a small fortune from trading cattle, charcoal, and groceries at a bush outpost. He later boasted to one reporter, ''I had 3,000 blacks working for me then.'' He was proud of his ability to get the locals to work and ran his life very much along the lines of those brutal slave masters in the deep South of the United States in the mid-1800s.

Ferreira was renowned for having a whole harem of black slave girls in those days. They would be expected to perform any duty he required at the flick of a finger. The colonial had an extensive collection of firearms and did not hesitate to use them when any of his workers disobeyed his orders.

He would frequently tell friends that he wanted to raise his own slave girls ''so that they do absolutely everything I want without question. It's better to catch them young and then mold them into precisely what one wants.''

Stories of Ferreira's brutal treatment of his slaves were commonplace. There were even rumors that he had a couple of ''favorites'' whom he kept shackled in a barn near his huge mansion. People reckoned that the bulky entrepreneur would use and abuse them whenever it took his fancy.

So, it was not really so surprising when Ferreira

heard about two unwanted babies in the local village and bought them for a pittance from their families. His sole intention was to bring them up as his personal slave girls. No one knows whether Ferreira paid the children's parents any actual cash for their babies. But then his power was such within that backward community that no one would have dared question his actions in any case.

Whenever any of the numerous other colonials confronted Ferreira about his actions, he told them, "No one else would have cared for them. They'd be dead inside a year if I hadn't taken them on."

And in the beginning, at least, he seemed to treat the two girls reasonably. However, the first thing he did was strip them both of their local native names and re-christen them Susana and Emilia.

"They're my property now and I'll call them whatever I like," Ferreira told one nosy neighbor in Angola.

For the next few years, Susana and Emilia were trained by Ferreira for their eventual duties as full-fledged slave girls. He wanted to ensure that they were obedient in every quarter. No task would be too much for them; he would make sure of that.

But then Angola gained its independence from Portugal in 1975. Somehow, he managed to smuggle the two girls with him back to Portugal, even though they had no passports.

Once home in the village of Sao Joao de Loure, Ferreira set the girls to work and forced them to live in a draughty outhouse while he, his wife, and three daughters lived in relative luxury in the main farm-house.

So, while Ferreira's children attended the local school, his young girl slaves were put to work each day from dawn until late at night, even though they were both still under the age of ten.

At night, Susana and Emilia were chained up on the straw-laden floor of the barn to prevent their escape. They were also kept on starvation rations that consisted of leftovers tipped into a bowl from which they both ate with their hands.

There were no toilet facilities in the outhouse so the girls would urinate and defecate like animals and occasionally one of Ferreira's farm workers would rake it all up.

Many of the other workers on the farm were aware of the girls' plight, but they did nothing for fear they would lose their jobs or face a violent backlash from heavyweight Ferreira.

Frequently the slave girls would be given no food at all. On other occasions, they would be taken out into the fields that surrounded the farm and told to eat animal fodder. When the girls complained, Ferreira used the cow dung as a deterrent.

But when the girls got to their early teens, Ferreira's intentions became more far-reaching. Sometimes he would appear drunk, unzip his pants, and insist they each perform oral sex on him.

Then he would try to have sex with one or both of the girls, but usually gave up because he was so drunk.

At night the girls were so cold that they would snuggle up alongside each other to keep warm. One time, Ferreira stumbled into the outhouse and tried to get them to perform sexual acts on each other. The poor, innocent slave girls had no idea of how to perform in front of their master.

If either of the girls ever objected to his sexual advances, Ferreira would get out his favorite bullwhip, force the offending girl to pull down her tattered trousers, and whip her on her bare behind. Then he would frequently commit some kind of sex act to prolong the obvious excitement he felt at beating them.

Ferreira's other favorite instruments of torture included a truncheon and a stave. Often he would punish the girls for no apparent reason other than because he gained some perverted delight from inflicting pain on them.

Worse still were the living conditions. As the girls hit their teens they continued to sleep on old straw, often soaked with urine, and virtually every night one or the other of them would be bitten by one of the dozens of rats that also lived in the barn. Susana still bears the scars from the beatings and rat bites to this day.

Both girls were forbidden from talking to the townspeople in Sao Joao de Loure, but they were sometimes sent out shopping. Fatima Abreu, a hairdresser, said later that their plight was obvious to anyone because of the cuts, bruises, and welts disfiguring their faces.

"It was a local scandal," she says. "But Ferreira was such a violent figure that people were afraid to offer the girls shelter."

In 1985, Emilia was claimed by her father, a Portuguese man who had known Ferreira in Angola. He took her to another village and tried to help her start a new life.

But Emilia could not escape the nightmarish memories of those awful years at the hands of Ferreira and she committed suicide just a few months after her "escape" from that horrendous life of slavery. It was crystal clear that she died of a broken heart.

She had complained to her family about constant nightmares and she desperately missed Susana, who had been her only friend in the world for virtually her entire life. In the end she felt she could not carry on.

Unaware of what had happened to her only friend, Susana had no choice but to stay with Ferreira. She was illiterate, unable to wash properly, and completely untrained for the outside world. She knew that Ferreira was a bad man, but she did not know where to go for refuge.

However, as she reached her late teens, Susana started to repeatedly question her situation. She was curious about life, and she determined that one day she would pick her moment and get away from evil Ferreira.

Meanwhile, her overweight master started to force himself upon her more and more regularly.

It was not until a few years later that she finally

plucked up the courage to flee his property and plead for sanctuary at the house of a local couple, hairdresser Fatima Abreu and her husband Antonio.

At first, Susana was too frightened to report her situation to the authorities. She feared that Ferreira would come after her and hunt her down in the way he always threatened he would if she ever ran away.

Eventually the Abreus persuaded Susana to take her story to the police, who finally charged Ferreira under a law prohibiting slavery.

"When Susana came here she was around 18, but she'd never been toilet trained, only knew how to eat with her hands, and was very traumatized psychologically," says Fatima Abreu.

The Susana of today is a very different person, even though her new home is just 200 meters from that of her one-time "owner" Ferreira. She often saw the fearsome farmer outside his house but has never exchanged a word with him since her escape.

Susana has now married and is brimming with hope and confidence for the future. But she has only just received the identity documents she needed to get married.

"I remember that my original African name was Kiumbi," she says. "Ferreira invented the name Susana, but for the 13 years I was with him I was only called 'nigger' and never addressed by any name at all."

As for Ferreira, a corpulent man in his late sixties, he spends most of his time sitting on his porch, brooding over what he sees as the injustice of the case against him.

Cursing the law and the press, he insists he did nothing wrong, though he openly admits he had beaten Susana on occasions as "punishment for stealing fruit from the neighbors."

He adds, "How could they could they try an old man like me? I spent a fortune bringing up those girls. I gave them everything and this is how they reward me."

Ferreira was eventually found guilty of enslaving Susana and her tragic friend Emilia and was sentenced to three years in prison.

6

HELP ME, PLEASE!

Whatever happens to them is happening inside the house, and what goes on inside the house is personal. In Kuwait, homes are traditionally and constitutionally sacred places.
 Ghanim al-Najjar, Kuwaiti human rights
 activist

———

Kuwaitis are surely among the most privileged and pampered people in history. With their vast oil wealth they simply hire people to do almost all their work.

Before the invasion by Iraq on August 2, 1990, 80 percent of the labor force was non-Kuwaiti, which meant there were two hundred thousand non-Kuwaiti servants in the country.

Every family had five or six servants, but after the invasion, the Kuwaitis decided for security reasons to reduce the number of foreigners in the country. Consequently, in October of 1991, the minister of the interior issued regulations limiting the number of servants a family could employ.

A family of five could have only two; a family larger than that could have four. Many Kuwaitis found the restrictions too harsh, however, and within a week the law was amended to allow a family to pay an annual fee if they wanted more servants.

So it was that Jenny Casanova from the Philippines came to be employed as a slave maid in Kuwait.

"Where are the children's shoes. *Where?*"

The mistress of the house was once again screaming at Jenny Casanova.

"I told you to put them in the cupboard. Where are they?"

Jenny looked nervously at her mistress. She had been through this so many times before, and she knew what was probably going to come next.

"I try to find them. I try," she pleaded with the woman.

Jenny moved out of the children's room to see if the shoes were in a cupboard in the hallway, but she felt the woman follow her.

"You stupid bitch. You lose everything!"

"But the children are always leaving them around the house," Jenny replied. It was a hasty response for the circumstances, and she knew what was coming next before she had even finished uttering her defiant reply.

The first punch connected with her lower abdomen. It was Jenny's mistress's favorite first "hit." She followed it up with a flurry of stinging slaps to the face. Jenny tried to cover her face with her hands to prevent the scratching she had suffered from her mistress's dark blood-red fingernails in the past. But the woman grabbed Jenny's wrist and pulled her hand down before smacking her hard on the cheeks.

"Please. Stop," pleaded Jenny.

But it was all to no avail. This was only the beginning.

Her mistress kept yelling. "You're useless. What do I pay you all this money for? You can't even find the children's shoes."

"All that money" consisted of $165 a month. Less than a third of the minimum wage in oil-rich Kuwait.

Just then the beating stopped, and the woman moved determinedly towards a cupboard further down the hall. Jenny slumped against the wall, relieved that her latest beating appeared to be over. She turned and headed back to the children's room.

Suddenly, she heard a whistling sound, then moments later felt a stinging sensation on her backside.

"You need to be taught a lesson, girl," her mistress screamed as she started whacking her slave girl with a cane.

The stick came down on Jenny with such force that it made her crouch in a corner of the hallway. Unfortunately this simply presented the women with an even clearer target.

She began thrashing Jenny on her backside and the back of her thighs. What seemed like dozens of hits followed.

As Jenny again crouched on the tiled floor to try

and roll herself up in a ball to avoid the worst, her skirt rode up, exposing more flesh to her mistress. It was like the proverbial red rag to a bull. The beating became even more intense.

"I will teach you to be insolent. How dare you answer me back. Only speak when spoken to. Do you understand?"

Jenny tried to nod her head in the hope that it might help persuade her mistress to stop the thrashing. Eventually she stopped because she seemed to be getting bored with inflicting that form of punishment.

"Don't move. Stay here," screamed her mistress.

Jenny shivered with fear as she watched her mistress go back to that cupboard where she had gotten the cane a few minutes earlier.

This time she emerged with a vacuum cleaner hose. As Jenny tried to scramble to her feet, the first excruciating swipe knocked her back down to the floor.

Jenny was hit at least a dozen more times before the mistress of the house decided she had made her point. The young slave was lying crumpled up on the floor, too scared to move in case it provoked yet another attack.

"Get up," said the mistress. "Get up—*now!*"

Jenny looked up at the angry, twisted face of her employer and tried to use the wall to support herself as she attempted to stand up.

"Get your dirty hands off my clean walls."

Jenny fell back onto the wall. She couldn't see properly through her tear-filled eyes, and the pain searing throughout the lower half of her body was appalling.

"I'll be back in five minutes and I expect you to have cleaned out the children's rooms," barked her mistress.

Another day had begun in the household from hell for domestic slave girl Jenny Casanova.

It all seemed a million miles away from the brightly colored streets of Manila, in the Philippines, where pretty, dark-haired, 30-year-old Jenny had lived until a year earlier.

With three daughters all under the age of ten and no job, she had actively sought work in Kuwait "for the future of my children."

Her first move was to join an employment agency that promised to place women in jobs in the wealthy Middle East for a $500 fee.

She was thrilled when the agency announced they had found her a family to work for in Kuwait City. Little did she realize she was about to begin a never-ending nightmare.

On her arrival at the impressive detached house in an immaculate, wealthy suburb, Jenny actually believed that she would be reasonably happy. And in any case, her salary would help pay for her children's upkeep back in Manila, and that was all that really mattered.

The master of the house was a civil servant who worked long hours, but his wife and their four children seemed the epitome of domestic family bliss.

She definitely felt a slight coldness toward her from all the family members, but she took that to be shyness and presumed they would all get along eventually.

But within hours of arriving, she was told that her salary would be withheld for at least the first two months to recover part of what the master of the house had paid to a Kuwait recruitment agency.

Jenny was a little disturbed by this but decided to get down to work on the basis that once that initial period was completed she could then send all her wages back to her needy family in Manila.

Jenny got up at 5:30 every morning to clean the house before the family woke. Her room was a tiny cubicle with just a mattress on the floor. Over the first few days, the mistress laid down some bizarre ground rules.

"You must only rest in your room when your duties are over," she barked.

A few days later, Jenny noticed that the mistress got very angry when she caught her husband talking to Jenny in the hallway.

"You talk to me only. Do you understand?"

Jenny nodded nervously. It soon became apparent that no one in that family was going to even give her the time of day. She noticed that the family dog got more attention.

Within a few weeks, her life was governed by a grueling pattern that consisted of rising before dawn and always working until at least midnight every day of the week. She had to do all the cooking and clean-ing and take care of four children aged 15, 14, 12, and six.

One day Jenny, a strict Catholic, asked her mistress if she could go to church.

"Filipinos don't go outside. Ever," came the reply.

Jenny sensed a great deal of tension creeping into her mistress's response.

Shortly after that she received the first of the reg-ular beatings that became a terrifying feature of life inside that house.

By the time of that dreadful thrashing inflicted be-cause she could not find the children's shoes, Jenny had reached the end of her tether.

As she crawled into the bathroom to try and tend to her wounds, she felt a wave of despair over her situation. She was trapped in a strange land without enough money to get home in a house dominated by a sadistic employer who had virtually threatened her with death if she dared to try and escape.

The mistress obviously sensed that Jenny was con-templating escape because later that same day she in-sisted that Jenny go with her to visit a sick relative. Clearly, she feared that Jenny might run away if left alone in the house.

"You have to leave before she kills you," one of the maids at that relative's house told Jenny as the two women sat down in the servants' quarters for a cup of tea while their mistresses talked upstairs.

Ironically, it was thanks to her employer taking her

to that other house that she built up the courage to leave.

The other maid had been so shocked to hear about the beatings and nonstop verbal abuse that she told Jenny to leave immediately, before she returned to the house and found herself trapped with nowhere to go.

Pointing to the driveway outside the house where they were, the other maid said, "Go to the gate slowly, then run."

She gave Jenny a dinar and hugged her.

"You have to do it."

Jenny left the house and hailed down a taxi which took her to the Philippine Embassy in the city. There she found more than two hundred other Philippine maids who had all fled their employers in Kuwaiti City. It was a virtual epidemic.

The reasons for the widespread mistreatment of maids in Kuwait and elsewhere are found partly in cultural traditions and values.

"First, it is because they are women, and women are mistreated generally in Kuwait," explains Eman al-Bedah, a Kuwaiti human rights activist. "Second, because they are maids. They are lower-class, and people exercise their power over them."

Bedah herself employs two Sri Lankan maids, but she allows them to attend regular religious services, and they may receive phone calls and have visits from friends. She is the exception.

"Our neighbors say we are spoiling them," says Bedah.

Much of the reporting of mistreatment in recent

years has focused on rape and sexual abuse by men, but it is actually the women responsible for supervising the slave maids who are guilty of the worst atrocities.

"Many of them are treating their maids the way their husbands treat them," says Bedah.

The status of women in Kuwait is marked by contradictions. Their political rights are severely restricted; they don't even have the right to vote, but the popular Western image of the veiled Arab woman, docile and subservient to her husband, doesn't apply in Kuwait.

But the Asian maids in Kuwait suffer from more than just being women in a male-dominated society. They are foreigners in an extremely closed and xenophobic society. No one is automatically entitled to citizenship unless they can prove their family has lived there since before 1920.

That leaves tens of thousands of essentially stateless people, many of whom were born in Kuwait and have lived their entire lives in the country, and whose fathers and grandfathers were born there, but who are not actual citizens. Even other Arabs are considered inferior by the Kuwaitis, and the maids, being Asians, are at the bottom of the heap.

"People don't see it as a problem; they don't think that many are mistreated," says Ghanim al-Najjar, a prominent human rights activist with a strictly pro-government opinion.

He even insists, "We have a lot of maids in this

country, and abuse and mistreatment are not very common.''

As for the failure of the Kuwaiti government to protect the maids, he says, ''Whatever happens to the maids is happening inside the house, and what goes on inside the house is personal. In Kuwait, homes are traditionally and constitutionally sacred places.'' In other words, it is not the business of the state to regulate anything that happens in the home.

He also says, ''It's very hard to know what really happened. If a maid says she's been beaten or neglected, how on earth can you prove that?''

Back at the Philippine Embassy in Kuwait City, Jenny Casanova nursed a black, blue, and yellow left eye— a direct result of that final beating from her mistress— as well as a large bruise on her upper right arm and bruises on her left calf and thigh.

Then to her horror she saw her mistress's husband being shown into an office next to the room where she was seated with dozens of other abused maids.

Jenny rushed to the embassy secretary sitting nearby.

''What's he doing here? He's not taking me back. Never.''

It then transpired that her former employer had come to the embassy to try and persuade Jenny to go to the employment agency that had brought her to Kuwait, so he could get back the money he had paid for her.

''I want my passport back first,'' demanded Jenny,

safe in the knowledge that neither he or his wife could do anything to harm her while she remained in the embassy.

The man, dressed in a long white robe and white headdress, pleaded with Jenny to accompany him to the recruitment agency.

"You have to help me. I want my money back."

But Jenny was in no mood to be helpful to the husband of the woman who had sadistically beaten her continually for months.

"I just want my passport."

It was a standoff that neither party could win. In the end the man stormed out of the embassy, having failed to get what he wanted. Then in an extraordinary outburst he insisted that Jenny had actually been the one hitting his wife.

"But my wife hit her back. She got what she deserved," added the man, before crossing the street and getting into a gold-colored Cadillac.

Jenny Casanova was just one of tens of thousands of young Asian women who come to Kuwait to find work and escape the poverty back at home.

The Kuwaiti government reckons there are 71,000 domestic servants from Asia, including 30,000 from India, 25,000 from the Philippines, 11,000 from Bangladesh, and 5,000 from Sri Lanka.

Almost none of them speak Arabic, and the language barrier frequently results in problems between employer and employee. Many of the maids are recruited by unscrupulous agencies that take their money without telling them what lies ahead, or even, in some cases, where they are going.

In Kuwait and throughout the Persian Gulf states, these women are taken advantage of by their employers: they are forced to work long hours for low pay, and are often virtually enslaved. They find that they have no place to go for protection. The Kuwaiti government offers them next to nothing, and their own embassies in Kuwait help them only grudgingly.

Many employers do not appreciate the situ ation because they consider it a matter of principle not to allow the slave maids to leave as they have paid out big money to agencies to get them in the first place.

The police station in the Dasma district of Kuwait City is a ramshackle three-story building, in which policemen in white robes lounge around on sagging vinyl-covered couches.

The Dasma police station has become a sort of informal complaint-resolution center for runaway slave maids. Between five and six o'clock most evenings, buses arrive from the embassies with maids who have fled the homes of employers.

Most of the women hope that the police can persuade their employers to return their passports and maybe even the money for a ticket home.

Virtually all of them claim to have been beaten and treated like slaves. But some of them even insisted they had been beaten by the woman who ran one particular recruitment agency after her employer had taken her back complaining that the maid did not work hard enough.

The Kuwaiti government recently enacted regulations to license the recruiting agencies, but these regulations are not likely to be enforced since the agencies are owned by Kuwaitis. And even though Kuwait does have laws against assault, they have not been enforced when a maid has been attacked by her employer.

Officials in the ministry of the interior, which has responsibility for maids, cannot provide any documentation that proves any man has ever been prosecuted for the rape of a maid or of a woman having been prosecuted for beating a maid; Philippine and Sri Lankan diplomats said that they were aware of no criminal prosecutions of employers for assaults on maids. It seems unlikely that the situation will change until the Kuwaitis themselves are willing to acknowledge the seriousness of the problem.

As if to prove that point, in 1993 Kuwait offered to fly home many of the abused slave/servants—at more than twice the regular airfare. The government said the additional costs were to provide Kuwaiti employers with a "reimbursement fee."

"We cannot afford this. We are stuck," says Yolanda Rodriguez, housemother to many of the women who have taken refuge at the Philippine Embassy.

"Our life is worth nothing to the Kuwaitis," says another abused servant, Marife Venzon.

7

THE ROOT OF ALL EVIL

All punishment is mischief. All punishment in itself is evil.
    Jeremy Bentham, author (1789)

———

Cynthia Montano wondered what the hell she was doing driving round the seediest part of this chaotic border town. But her employer, Santee Kimes, had been most insistent that she wanted two more girls *immediately*, and Cynthia knew it was more than her job was worth not to find Kimes two new slaves.

The rental car was not conspicuous despite the California plates because Tijuana was literally swarming with visitors who had popped across the border for a taste of the cheap local liquor and women.

As Cynthia turned down a side street she spotted two young girls who looked perfect. ''Make sure they don't wear makeup or jewelry,'' Santee Kimes had told her before she set off from the Kimes's impres-

75

sive mansion in La Jolla, California, just 40 miles from the border with Mexico.

"And they have to be very subservient," were Kimes's last words as Cynthia drove off in her rental Ford.

Now, just two hours later, she seemed to have found exactly what her mistress required.

Cynthia slowed the car down and the electric window slid open quietly.

"*¿Hola. Comó estan?*"

The two girls looked up smiling. They couldn't have been much more than 14 or 15.

Cynthia got out of the car and started her own gentle interrogation of the two prospective slaves. But one of the girls seemed uneasy. She told Cynthia that her parents would never let her just leave town for a job in California. Cynthia's heart sank. She knew that both girls had to be entirely willing at the outset, otherwise it could create problems later.

She left the two girls on the sidewalk and continued her prowl for new recruits for her mistress.

Cynthia was only too well aware that she would get a severe beating from Santee Kimes back in her beachside villa in La Jolla, near San Diego, if she did not deliver two slave girls.

Santee Kimes was a very strange woman. Her mood swings had become notorious in the Kimes household. One minute she would be charming, then the next she would snap into violence that was all too often directed at her servants—and that included Cynthia.

"I prefer them healthy, young, and easy to manipulate," Kimes had often told Cynthia, who suspected that some of the girls were sexual fantasy figures to Kimes, even though she had never witnessed any sexual attacks upon the women in the household.

Cynthia had watched Kimes's anticipation whenever new slave girls were recruited as "domestic servants" in one of Kimes's numerous households spread across America. She suspected that at the very least the girls provided some kind of fantasy kick for Kimes and her husband Kenneth.

Back on the tatty streets of Tijuana that warm evening, Cynthia continued her hunt for new slaves for her mistress. Less than an hour later she spotted another pair of girls slightly older than the previous ones and started her patter once again.

It emerged that the two girls were just out of school, unemployed but desperate for work and particularly keen on the idea of a fresh start across the border in cash-rich California. They were perfect.

Cynthia drove them to their parents' homes and explained the deal. She told them that the girls would be working for a very nice lady as maids at her vast homes. It seemed like a dream come true to the families who were struggling to exist.

"We'll organize your papers once we get to La Jolla," explained Cynthia to the bewildered girls before she opened the trunk of the Ford. "But it's best if you hide in here while we get across the border."

The girls looked at each other and giggled. It was an adventure, and they had each other for protection.

What harm could possibly come to them?

Two hours later, Cynthia rolled up outside the Kimes's whitewashed villa-style residence just a stone's throw from the Pacific Ocean with her two new recruits.

Santee Kimes did indeed lick her lips like the cat who'd found the cream when she saw the two young girls walking up to the house.

"Well, well," she purred. "They look perfect."

Kimes told Cynthia to take the two girls to their room, a tiny box-shaped place with just one single mattress for them both to sleep on.

When one of the girls complained, Cynthia told them that they would be given their own rooms within a few days, but for the moment they would have to make do.

"Is it possible to eat something?" asked one of the girls.

"Tomorrow. You must sleep first."

At 5:30 the next morning, the two girls were shaken by Cynthia.

"It's time to work. Come on."

Neither of them stirred at first. Then Santee Kimes appeared, hands on her hips, looking every inch the matriarchal mistress.

"Get up. *Now!*"

The girls tried to pull down their skimpy T-shirts as they scrambled to their feet.

"Move your butts. Get to it," screeched the mistress.

* * *

On the face of it, Santee Kimes was a most unlikely abuser of slaves. This attractive 41-year-old dark-haired wife to hotel chain owner Kenneth Kimes seemed to have everything she ever needed at her fingertips.

Her millionaire husband provided her with homes in La Jolla, Las Vegas, Hawaii, Washington, D.C., and Cancun, Mexico. She had expensive cars, designer label clothes, and he allowed her to employ at least six servants at any one time.

But beneath the veneer of respectability lay an ever-growing fear of the outside world on the part of Santee Kimes.

She hated her husband's relatives, whom she called "creeps," and became increasingly paranoid about them wanting to abduct her 10-year-old son.

"They travelled a great deal, moving from place to place to assure themselves privacy," explains Santee Kimes's devoted friend, retired California law enforcement officer Grant Christopherson. "Sometimes they registered under different names to make sure their enemies—the creeps—were not aware of where Santee was."

Those fears of abduction, Kimes later claimed, were why she was so secretive and strict with her domestic servants.

Kimes even told her friend Grant Christopherson that someone had tried to grab her son while they were walking on a beach in Hawaii, but that Kimes had fought the assailant off and he ran away.

"There was also one episode when someone broke

into her household in Hawaii and used what looked like blood to paint threatening signs on the wall," adds Christopherson.

The law enforcement officer even recalls how Kimes told him that she "went into her car, closed the door, and discovered rattlesnakes in the car. She couldn't get the door open and had to break the window to get out."

The cause of all Kimes's fear and tension seems to have been her husband's business practices.

"Her husband was a very wealthy man, and apparently money was the name of the game," explains Christopherson's wife Patricia. In short, Kenneth Kimes appeared to be mixing with some pretty tough fellows.

Kimes's numerous servants hired throughout the early and mid-1980s had no doubt they were being held as slaves.

Adela Sanchez Guzman found herself trapped inside the Kimes home in Hawaii. She was locked in her tiny bedroom at night and told that she was forbidden to leave the property for any reason.

And when another maid was hired shortly after they arrived in Hawaii, Adela was forbidden from even speaking to the girl.

When Santee Kimes spotted the two women talking a few days later she went berserk and beat Adela with a wooden coat hanger.

"I told you not to speak to her. I told you," Kimes kept repeating over and over again as she beat her slave girl.

Then she grabbed a wire coat hanger and made Adela remove her jeans "just to make sure you never forget my orders ever again."

When Adela began crying, Kimes shouted at her, "You can't leave here. You are going to be here forever."

But that was just the first of numerous beatings at the hands of her mistress. Kimes slapped Adela around the head and face virtually every day.

She would get particularly infuriated whenever she found Adela crying in her room.

As the weeks turned into months, Kimes got into the habit of beating her slave girls whenever it took her fancy. Then one day, Kimes found a piece of paper containing the address of the house. She was even more furious.

"Come here, girl," she screamed in Adela's direction.

The terrified slave girl hesitantly moved toward her mistress.

"What is this?"

"Nothing," came the reply.

"Nothing? It is our address. I think you were planning to give it to someone so that you could leave."

"No, señora."

"Yes, señora. You were planning to escape. I told you. You will never get away from here, so do not try."

Santee Kimes's nostrils flared. She ripped open the drawer of a nearby desk and took out a man's belt.

"Lay your hand on the desk."

"What?"

Kimes grabbed Adela's tiny wrists and smashed her hands down on the desk.

"Don't move."

The first lash on her hand was the most painful. After that, everything seemed a blur.

In November, 1984, Kimes and her three current slave/maids travelled from her luxurious home in Hawaii to yet another family residence in Las Vegas.

One day, 21-year-old slave girl Maribel Cruz Ramirez was ironing her mistress's clothes when Kimes discovered a slip of paper with the telephone number of a maid she had met in Hawaii.

"Why the fuck have you got that, girl?" Kimes barked.

"It is my friend's number, señora."

"I told you not to talk to anyone. Why have you defied me?"

Maribel was stunned. She knew what this was leading toward, and she did not know how to handle it.

"Take off your clothes. *Now*!"

Maribel hesitated. Then Kimes picked up the red-hot iron and held it close to the slave girl's face. She was too frightened to speak.

Kimes then held the iron just above the girl's thigh and started to move it up ever so slowly.

"Do it!"

Maribel began unbuttoning her blouse. She watched as Kimes put the iron down and plugged it back in the socket.

''Faster, girl. Faster!''

When it came to her panties, Maribel hesitated.

''Everything.''

Standing there completely naked, the frightened servant feared the worse.

Just then Kimes unplugged the iron.

Maribel covered her face with her hands and began to weep.

''Shut up!'' screamed Kimes.

She held up the iron and pressed it against the back of Maribel's hands.

''Don't ever talk to anyone again. D'you understand, girl?''

''Yes, señora. Yes,'' whimpered the slave girl.

Then she put the iron down one more time and dragged the girl along the corridor to the master bedroom. Maribel was too scared to manage any resistance by this stage.

Kimes threw the naked girl on the bed.

''Don't move.''

Then Kimes ripped open the door of her walk-in closet and pushed some of her clothes to one side.

She walked back to the young girl, grabbed her by the wrists once more, and forced her into the closet.

''This is your bed for tonight. If you try to leave, I will kill you.''

Maribel watched in fear as the closet door slid shut. She could hear her mistress walking around the room.

''Just remember what I said. I don't want to hear a word from you.''

Maribel collapsed on the floor of the closet. She

was too afraid to take any of her mistress's clothes to use as a bed, so she lay on the splintered wooden floor, naked, cold, and miserable.

A couple of hours later, she heard Kimes giggling as she entered the bedroom with her husband. Maribel had no choice but to listen to their heated lovemaking. Her twisted mistress apparently was making a particularly loud noise because she knew that one of her maids was locked naked in the closet.

Throughout this period it became clear to all those working in the Kimes household that Santee Kimes was becoming increasingly paranoid as well as horrendously sadistic.

She insisted that she didn't want anyone in her house answering the door because she feared she was going to be served with a subpoena, but she never actually said what it related to.

"If people came to the door," explains Melody Keltz, who was hired as a tutor for Kimes's son, "Mrs. Kimes said I should not answer. If someone approached me outside, I was to say I was a decorator. She said someone was trying to serve and her husband with some kind of legal summons. I was not to let the maids open the door, not to let them mail letters, and not to let them leave the property. Mrs. Kimes said I should treat the maids like little children. She said they were stupid."

One time a maid got chicken pox and another tutor called Brownie Otto took her to a doctor. When Kimes found out she went berserk and beat both of them.

On another occasion, Kimes decided to show Otto "how to treat the maids."

She went into the backyard of the vast house in Las Vegas where one maid was working and grabbed her by the hair and started shaking her.

Otto looked on in astonishment as Kimes gave her own running commentary.

"See? They don't respond. They are just so dumb."

Then Otto was stunned when Kimes pulled the struggling maid over her knees and ripped open her jeans before pulling them down. She then proceeded to spank her bare bottom at least half a dozen times. It appeared that she was deriving some kind of sexual pleasure from the beating.

Melody Keltz left Kimes soon after another similar incident because "I was not valued as a human being by her." She later claimed she did nothing to report Kimes's brutal regime to the authorities because she feared that Kimes would kill her.

Meanwhile, another maid, Dolores Vasquez, age 17, was beaten, scalded with hot water, and threatened with a gun by Kimes.

One beating was caused when the young slave girl burnt some toast. A few days later Kimes pulled a loaded pistol on the attractive brunette maid and tried to force it in her mouth before being interrupted by the doorbell. A third incident occured in a hotel suite while the slave girl was accompanying her mistress on a trip.

Dolores explains, "I had an allergy and my blood

pressure rose and I fainted. La señora said to go into the bathroom.'' Kimes then forcibly stripped the girl of her clothes and pushed her into the steaming hot shower. ''I put the water to lukewarm and she changed the water to very hot. It burned. When I moved away to a corner of the bathtub, she threw hot water on me with a little pot.''

One time, yet another of Kimes's son's tutors was stunned to discover she was expected to help her employer smuggle more slave girls across the border.

Teresa Richards actually asked a cab driver in Tijuana to take her to a quiet crossing point where she saw a gap in the border fence and walked two prospective maids across the border.

Richards later explained, ''Mrs. Kimes told me to treat the maids as if they were chairs. They were to be allowed no freedom.''

The tutor claimed she was virtually brainwashed with the fear that Kimes would go after her if she dared to leave her employment.

One of the few slave girls to get away from Kimes was feisty young Maria Salgado. She was just 14 years old when Kimes picked her up in Mexico and offered her a job as a maid.

Within days of arriving in California, Maria was hit in the face by Kimes, who objected to the way that the young girl had answered her back on a point of discipline.

When Maria tried to find a telephone in the house to call her family she discovered part of it in a bureau drawer, and another part in a closet. She was just about to put the instrument together and plug it in when Kimes came in and immediately punished her with a severe beating on her backside.

Two days later Maria broke a window and fled the house in La Jolla. She then reported her captivity to police officers and was eventually reunited with her parents.

The FBI, acting on information provided by Maria, arrested Kenneth and Santee Kimes at their La Jolla home in the summer of 1985.

Santee Kimes faced a trial in February of 1986. But just a few weeks before the case got under way, she escaped from the lockup section of the Southern Nevada Memorial Hospital, where she was undergoing medical tests.

Kimes was eventually re-arrested after four days on the run when U.S. marshalls and FBI agents tracked her down to the parking lot of the Elbow Room Bar in Las Vegas. She had spent her nights on the run sleeping under trees and any other place she could escape the elements.

In a precedent-setting case in Nevada, Kimes was found guilty on 14 of 16 counts of holding young women as slaves after the jury took nine hours deliberating its verdict.

"Santee Kimes is a greedy, cunning, and cruel woman who thought she was above the law," assistant U.S. attorney Karla Dobinski told the court in her closing statement. "She lied to the maids to get them to go with her. She coerced them to stay with her by overcoming their will."

Calling it one of the most unusual cases he has ever presided over, U.S. District Judge Howard McKibben sentenced Kimes to the maximum five-year prison term.

But he placed her husband, Kenneth Kimes, 67, on probation, suspending a three-year term except for a 60-day period in an alcohol treatment center, and imposed a $70,000 fine.

Judge McKibben told Santee Kimes it was obvious "you have some fairly deep-seated emotional and psychological problems."

He said reports from a government-appointed psychiatrist as well as another psychiatrist both indicated the woman was in need of therapy.

Noting that Kimes "suffered from fairly substantial emotional disturbances," he said that had to be balanced against the "reprehensible acts" for which she was convicted.

In July, 1991, the enslavement conviction against Santee Kimes was upheld by a federal appeals court.

Kimes has now been freed and is believed to be living in California.

8

THE EL MONTE SWEATSHOP

He who is by nature not his own but another's man, is by nature a slave.
    Aristotle

In the dense predawn mist, no one noticed the slight figure scrambling carefully over the razor-wired wall of the backyard of the nondescript apartment block on a busy suburban street. The only noise was the occasional distant purr of a truck carrying some early-shifters on their way to work.

"WELCOME TO FRIENDLY EL MONTE," read the baby-blue-on-yellow sign planted at the curb in front of the apartment complex. Inside, scores of slave girls were living a life of fear and loathing, beaten if they tried to complain about conditions.

Mariwan's heart was beating at a furious rate. The seconds had been ticking away since the pretty young

Thai woman had awakened and slipped silently out of the first floor window of the degrading dormitory that had been her squalid home since arriving in California from Thailand almost three years earlier.

Just a few hours before, Mariwan had set out her escape plan in very cold and calculating terms. She had just been beaten by the foreman called "Pa" at the horrendous sweatshop where she had been enslaved since the day her feet touched American soil. This time she had truly had enough. She had to do something to close this hellhole down before somebody died.

All thoughts of the so-called American dream had long since disappeared. Mariwan, age 26, and the 71 other women slaves at the sweatshop just wanted to go home to their families.

Their mistresses and masters were known by a variety of sick and twisted nicknames that would haunt the slave girls for the rest of their lives. There was "Auntie," the evil elderly Thai woman who would take great pleasure in beating many of them with a stick. Then there was the awful "Torn," supported by the pock-marked "Porn" and a host of others. The men would often take turns abusing their slaves.

On other occasions, the slave girls were proudly shown photographs of beaten women who had dared to try and escape from the El Monte labor camp. Many of the girls were told that if they disobeyed the regime inside the sweatshop they would be raped by Americans or Mexicans.

Some women were warned that their families

would have their homes in Thailand destroyed if they did not obey their orders to work in these labor camps. Slave girls had even been forced to carry out do-it-yourself dental work on their own teeth.

Runaway Mariwan had concluded that anything was better than this living nightmare, and even though she risked incarceration for having no legal travel documents, this was the only answer. Naturally, Mariwan was worried that the bosses of the factory might come after her, but she knew there would be no turning back after she had made her escape.

Once in the alley behind the apartment block, she continued running quietly along the edge of the wall, determined not to fail at the last hurdle. Mariwan thought she heard voices behind her, but it might have been from another building; it was impossible to tell. She just kept running.

The story that she had to tell authorities sounded almost too incredible for words, considering the location was a quiet town in the most civilized nation on earth.

But in the end they believed her and mounted a raid on the premises to liberate the slave girls and bring their masters and mistresses to justice.

The route that led to the sweatshop in El Monte, near Los Angeles, was, tragically, an all-too-familiar setup: Young Thai women were persuaded to pay unscrupulous agents in their homeland for travel and immigration documents with the promise of safe, secure, well-paid jobs on their arrival in the U.S.

Instead they were hearded into buses at L.A.'s International Airport and taken directly to the El Monte sweatshop and coerced into working.

Once the workers arrived at the so-called factory, the sweatshop bosses seized their passports and took back the "show money" that had been provided to them as cover should immigration officials question them about their planned tourist itineraries.

"It soon became crystal clear that they were working in a virtual labor camp," says one investigator who took part in the initial raid on the building.

Not only were the workers prevented from leaving the premises, but their slave masters and mistresses barred them from communicating with one another. The workers themselves actually believed they were working off travel debts of $5,000.

They were held in the guarded complex and forced to work from 7 A.M. to midnight, seven days a week for less than $2 an hour, and that money was simply deducted from their supposed debts to their masters.

According to many of the slave girls, it was always boiling hot inside the factory, where they were expected mainly to sew seams and collars, Hawaiian shirts, and surfer shorts. In the words of the most serious of the charges that their mistresses and masters would eventually face, "they were unlawfully inveigled, decoyed, seized, confined, kidnapped, and abducted" to their jobs from hell.

Yet El Monte itself could not be more removed from the sort of place where slavery thrived with such intensity and, apparently, little concern from the local population.

This working-class community of 110,000 prided itself on functioning more like a family than a city. When wagon train pioneers from the Midwest came looking for gold in the 1850s, El Monte was their oasis. The early settlement, bordered by Rio Hondo and the San Gabriel River, was lush with a plentiful water supply and vegetation. It became known as "El Monte, the end of the Santa Fe Trail."

Yet for those 72 slave girls who toiled in a factory disguised as an apartment block, it was hell.

The town where most children attended El Monte High School, married their sweethearts, and settled down to lead long, simple lives, chose to turn its back on the poor, innocent women entrapped by nine evil slave masters.

But then 1995 wasn't a good year for El Monte. The discovery of the sweatshop was only the latest high-profile news to tarnish the city's reputation. In February, a guest home for the mentally ill came under fire after one resident beat another to death with a rock.

Then in April, five people, including an infant and a five-year-old girl, were shot to death execution-style in their home.

Even after the discovery of the sweatshop—one of the biggest forced-labor camps ever uncovered in peacetime—local officials insisted that it could have been set up anywhere.

"There is nothing in El Monte that contributed to

this happening here,'' says John Leung, chairman and chief executive officer of the Titan Group, a minority-owned local development organization.

Yet others in the community were outraged that the sweatshop went unnoticed for so long.

''How the hell could no one have noticed it? The place was surrounded in razor-wire. I don't think anyone wanted to know about a bunch of Thais,'' reckons one local resident.

Local police chief Wayne Clayton defends his 131-member police force, saying his officers lacked the authority to go door-to-door inspecting every business. ''That sweatshop was housed very close to the corner on Santa Anita Avenue, one of our busiest streets. Nobody recognized it. When you drive by, you can almost step over it.''

Two weeks after the raid on the El Monte sweatshop, a federal grand jury indicted nine alleged operators of the slave business, charging that the forced-labor ring recruited workers in Thailand, smuggled them into the United States, confined them under threat, censored their mail, and monitored their telephone calls.

All nine defendants were charged with conspiracy and concealing and harboring illegal immigrants. The accused could face up to five years in prison and $250,000 fines on each of the charges.

Among those charged were a fugitive called Sukit Manasurangkul, age 40, who, the indictment stated, helped recruit the workers in Thailand. An arrest warrant was issued for this alleged recruiter, known to some workers as "Sunshine," who is still believed to be on the run in Thailand.

Seven of the suspects are said to be related, including four who may be the sons of the woman believed to be the ringleader—Suni Manasurangkul, 65, whom workers referred to as "Auntie." She allegedly ran the El Monte operation in matriarchal style, giving her slave girls working and sleeping assignments and warning them that they were not free to leave. She would often resort to violence if any of the women defied her.

Others in custody included two alleged guards at the El Monte complex and two women believed to be daughters-in-law of the evil Manasurangkul.

Within a month of the raid, U.S. and Californian officials filed lawsuits claiming some $5 million in back wages due to the former workers, who were freed from immigration custody within a week of the swoop. They are expected to serve as key witnesses in the criminal case against the sweatshop operators.

Others charged were Tavee Uvawas, 35; Sunton Rawungchaisong, 30; Rampa Suthaparasit, 32; Suporn Verayutwilai, 29; Seree Granjapiree, 28; Hong Wangdee, and Thanes Panthong, 30.

Incredibly, it was then disclosed that many of Los Angeles's most successful garment manufacturers had actually used the sweatshop to make goods.

Some retailers reacted strongly within days of hearing that they might be stocking garments made in the sweatshop.

"We will not tolerate conditions identified during

the El Monte raid,'' declared Bernard F. Brennan, chairman and chief executive officer of Montgomery Ward, the largest privately held retailer in the U.S., which immediately removed all the sweatshop's merchandising from sales floors nationwide. Other stores soon followed suit.

In contrast to the deplorable conditions of the El Monte sweatshop, the workers were housed in a fully equipped detention center following the raid on the ''factory.''

Immigration and Naturalization Service spokesman Ron Rogers says, ''They're getting three hot meals a day and a bed, and medical treatment is available.''

The most tragic aspect of the El Monte sweatshop is that there are millions more women where these came from. They are all too often poor, rural, single, and defenseless. There is always a Mr. Big lording it over them, a pimp, whether or not they work in the sex trade. It might be a cruel employer, a corrupt cop, a mindless bureaucrat—or even a parent.

Even when one of them managed to slip out of that razor-wired hellhole no one really wanted to be hear her story initially.

Now these women's accounts are going to be heard. They will get their day in court and many of them have already gotten new, legal jobs in California.

''They want to be as independent and self-sufficient as possible,'' explains Chanchanit Martorell, executive director of the Thai Community

Development Center, one of a handful of civilian groups who helped look after the slave girls following their liberation.

"It's been really hard for them to stay idle because they're so used to working," he says.

Some of the slave girls even returned to garment factories. Others asked for work in domestic service. The Thai community center helped to place the workers in new jobs and screened each potential post to ensure it offered at least the minimum wage and a safe environment.

The women also savored their first taste of freedom in the U.S. with visits to Disneyland and a specially held beachfront barbecue in Malibu.

Federal agents then swooped in on three more suspected sweatshops in the Los Angeles area and arrested 55 people including 39 Thai workers.

Interviews with workers at the sites produced definite evidence of minimum wage, overtime, child labor, and record-keeping violations, according to labor investigators.

The U.S. immigration service believes that the Thai nationals at these three new sites were also smuggled in and employed in a form of debt.

All three sweatshops were in largely immigrant areas of downtown Los Angeles, and officials claim that many of the workers appeared to have been "coached in what to say" by their supervisors.

But the El Monte and subsequent raids appear to have highlighted a huge problem in southern California, where there are estimated to be more than

100,000 workers being underpaid in the highly competitive garment industry.

Meanwhile, the reverberations from the El Monte raid continue to rumble.

California Governor Pete Wilson got involved when he demanded that U.S. Attorney General Janet Reno investigate the alleged indifference of the U.S. Immigration and Naturalization Service and the U.S. Attorney's Office in Los Angeles for their failure to close down the El Monte sweatshop sooner.

But as one legitimate Thai businessman in L.A. commented, "We all know this is just the tip of the iceberg. The sweatshops are everywhere and a few raids aren't going to get rid of them overnight."

9

CASUALTY OF WAR

This is what it means/to be a slave: to be abused and bear it,/compelled by violence to suffer wrong.
> Euripides, 425 B.C.

────────

Meiram was just 14 years old when she found herself orphaned after Sudanese nomads armed with machine guns and grenade launchers attacked her home village in the south of this desolate country.

As the young girl fled north with her sister and grandmother they were captured by another group of armed nomads, or Murahaleen, as they are known locally. Meiram managed to escape their clutches after one of the soldiers raped her and then fell asleep. She could hear other militiamen doing the same to her sister and grandma, but she knew she had to run for her life. The guilt of leaving behind her only two relatives would stay with her forever.

After three days of wandering through the desert, Meiram came across another band of nomads. At first she presumed they would abuse her like all the others, but this group actually seemed more civilized than those she had previously encountered.

They let her share their water and food and expected nothing in return. She rode their camels as they progressed through the desert and for the first time in many months she actually started to believe that life was worth living after all.

One of the leaders of the nomads called himself Bona and he seemed particularly concerned with Meiram's welfare. Whenever any of the other nomads took anything more than a passing interest in the young girl, he would ward them off gallantly.

Meiram actually felt she had found a family to replace the one she presumed had been so brutally killed during the earlier attack.

Bona gave Meiram back her respect. She began to gain some self-confidence, and he even started to help her to read and write as the band of nomads progressed though the southern part of the country.

At night, Meiram was allowed to sleep alone and Bona even issued a warning to all the other nomads not to try and sleep with her; otherwise, they would have to face his fury. Many of the younger nomads believed that Meiram was being "kept fresh" for Bona to have later when he reached his final destination.

But when the Murahaleen reached a busy desert town, Meiram noticed that Bona started barking orders at her to make herself look perfectly groomed.

"You must look clean and healthy in such a place
as this, otherwise the other women will look down on
you," he assured her in a fatherly fashion.

But Bona was actually preparing Meiram to be sold
as a slave girl to the highest bidder.

She did not even realize what was happening until
it was too late. Bona never spoke to her again. She
saw his self-satisfied face as she was taken away by
two male servants who worked for her new "owner,"
a steely eyed Arab called Mahmoud who had paid
Bona 4,000 Sudanese pounds (about $300) for her.

To make matters even worse, the town where she
had been stranded was right in the middle of the combat zone in Sudan's seven-year-old civil war.

"I felt betrayed, alone, and terrified. In the previous
few months I had lost my family, my self-respect, my
dignity, and now my freedom," recalls Meiram.

To start with, the young slave girl was expected to
wash and clean for her new master, living under the
constant fear of being killed if she did not work efficiently enough.

She received no money and precious little food
other than occasional scraps from the remains of the
servants' meals.

When there was a distribution of relief food for the
nation's millions of starving people nearby, Meiram's
master forbade her to attend.

The only thing she had held onto was her body.
For he made no attempt to molest her and she was at
least thankful for that.

But in an effort to get some real food, Meiram was forced to go and beg in the nearby market, which only opened when the bombing raids ceased. She would humbly hold out a begging bowl for hours on end and be extremely lucky if she raised enough money to buy a piece of fruit.

Back at her master's home, she was becoming increasingly withdrawn and unresponsive to his orders. Mahmoud started to beat her regularly with a stick. But his punishment created a twisted turn of good fortune for the young girl because he would feel so guilty afterwards that he'd let her have the pick of the fruit bowl once he had gorged it himself.

Although Meiram did not realize it, slavery had become a common occurrence in the Sudan in the late 1980s. Firsthand accounts from the southern Dinka people suggested that the classical ingredients of slavery—from capture to unpaid labor to beatings and sale—were widespread.

Young girl slaves, many not even yet in their teens, were bought and sold like cattle for purely sexual purposes as Meiram was about to find out.

For when the Arab decided to move on to the town of Arok, he took her with him and decided to buy himself another young girl as well.

''You look too tatty and thin to be the sort of slave girl I really want,'' he told Meiram. It seemed that his meanness toward her had actually saved her from having to make the ultimate sacrifice.

But when they got to Arok, Mahmoud could not find a suitable girl. Meiram became understandably

Gary Heidnik imprisoned five women in the cellar of his home and turned them into sex slaves, hoping to father a child by each of them. (AP/World Wide)

The body of Cindy Wellington is removed from the shallow grave where Heidnik had buried her. (AP/World Wide)

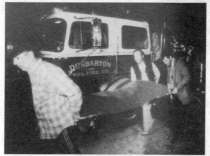

Officials from the Philadelphia Medical Examiner's Office remove the body parts that were found in Heidnik's refrigerator. (AP/World Wide)

"Jackie" Suphonphan Wood, the beautiful, cold, and calculating madam who enslaved Thai girls in Rosemead, California. (L.A. County Sheriff's Dept.)

Wood's Vietnamese lover Tai Thahn Pham, who subjected the girls to continuous physical abuse before the couple was arrested in 1994. (L.A. County Sheriff's Dept.)

The Los Angeles County Sheriff's Asian Organized Crime Unit, who successfully uncovered Wood's illicit sex slave business. Top, left to right, Sgt. Thomas Budds, Det. Jess Bembry, Det. William Howell, Det. Basil North. Bottom, left to right: Det. Hugh Lloyd, Det. Michael Soop, Det. Michael McGravy, Det. Juergin Franks, Det. Duncan Jefferys. (L.A. County Sheriff's Dept.)

An envelope filled with cash, found after the police raided Wood's brothel. (L.A. County Sheriff's Dept.)

One of the bedrooms in the house where the Thai girls were forced to have sex with hundreds of men. (L.A. County Sheriff's Dept.)

The comfortable house on nearby Hampton Avenue, where Wood and her lover Pham lived when they were not supervising the brothel. (Wensley Clarkson)

Helen Samuels, who suffered years of torture in the quiet London suburb of Bexleyheath, holds up the ragged clothes she was forced to wear throughout her incarceration. (*The Mail on Sunday*)

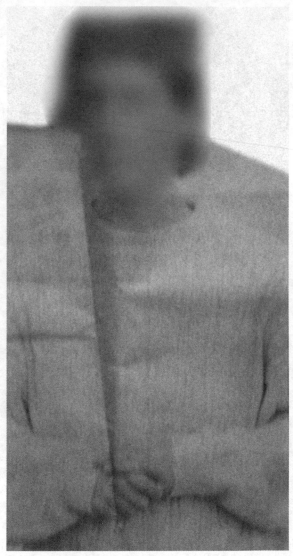

Glynis Edmunds, who was kidnapped and abused in London after agreeing to marry a stranger in exchange for a fee. (*News of the World*)

Evil madam Camille Simmons-Ruiz—known as Randi to her clients—buys sex slaves from agents in southeast Asia and then forces them to work as prostitutes in London. (*News of the World*)

Myra Ling-Ling Forde was recently exposed for running a sex slave business in a quiet English country town. (*The Sunday Mirror*)

Slave girl Viola (above), who suffered humiliation and degradation in a suburb of New Jersey for more than two years at the hands of her mistress, Mir (right). (Viola Johnson, Mir)

concerned. She felt torn because she did not want to be his sex slave, but she also felt that no other girl deserved that role either.

However, in the end she had no choice.

On the second night of their stay in Arok, her Arab master was sleeping in his own tent and she was sleeping with just a sheet for cover outside. Ever since their arrival in the town, she had barely slept a wink for fear that he might try to rape her during the night.

"I was so confused and scared. I did not want to submit to his demands but I needed him to survive. I just prayed that he would not come after me," she says.

About 4 A.M., Meiram finally fell into a troubled sleep. Her only weapon of defense was a stone she had picked on the roadside the previous day.

"Don't move. Just lie still," a harsh, smelly breath whispered.

Meiram tried to move, but he had her pinned down. She struggled for breath. His hand went over her mouth.

"Quiet!"

As her eyes adjusted to the dark she could just make out the face. It wasn't her master. But then a voice came out of the dark.

"Hurry up. Get a move on."

That was definitely her master. She tried to move her head to the side where his voice was coming from. She just caught a glance of him out of the corner of her eye before the man above her forced her head round straight again.

"Don't move, slave girl."

Just then, frightened Meiram became aware that at least three pairs of eyes were watching her in the darkness. She had just become the sex toy to three evil men, including her master.

For the following three months, Meiram was passed from man to man, often expected to sleep with all three in one evening. They fed her food continually in an effort to fatten her up. At first she could not resist the food, but she soon realized that the fatter she got the better they liked her, she started to secretly spit it out once they were out of sight. But it was especially hard to spit out the tasty meat and vegetables since she was so hungry much of the time.

Meiram later discovered that Mahmoud had intended to use her as his sex slave with the two other men all along. But he had agreed not to sleep with her until the other two men joined him and paid their share of her purchase price.

One of the other men treated her particularly roughly and would try to perform appalling acts of degradation on her on virtually a nightly basis.

Sometimes Mahmoud would show an almost sympathetic side by warning the man not to hurt her, but Meiram realized that he was only trying to protect his "investment." She knew that the day would eventually come when they would try to sell her on to other men.

She even heard them saying one day that with any

luck they could get at least what they paid for her back because she was still so young.

In every town they passed through, Meiram lived in fear of being sold to an even more brutal group of men. At least these three fed her, and after Mahmoud's intervention, the nastiest of the men had stopped forcing her to have painful, unlubricated anal sex.

The situation was not helped by the fact that the Sudanese government continued to arm virtually all its northern nomadic tribesmen, notably the Rizeigat and Misseriya, creating Wild West-type shootouts on a regular and terrifying basis.

Reports by the human rights organizations Africa Watch and Amnesty International provided evidence that such tribesmen had been armed to the teeth and given intelligence information about rival nomads by various government departments seeking to win Sudan's civil war on the cheap.

By encouraging attacks on people such as the Dinka, the government in Khartoum sought to debilitate a group that provided crucial support for the rebel Sudanese People's Liberation Army.

But none of this mattered to poor, innocent, young Meiram. Her only priority was to survive in the desert. She had even taken to wrapping herself in double the amount of clothing to try and hide her shapely figure in the hope it might put off her three masters.

However, they were not that easily dissuaded. Their nightly demands continued unabated.

During stopovers in towns, Meiram heard stories

from other slaves about even worse situations than the one she found herself in.

One Dinka man told her how he had been captured and sold twice, first for 100 Sudanese pounds (about $7), then for $220. He claimed that his second buyer castrated him and branded him with an iron used to brand cows. The man assured Meiram that many other Dinka men had been castrated.

In the Sudan, the prices of slaves followed very basic rules of supply and demand. Greatest demand—as in the nineteenth century when trading in slaves and ivory wrought widespread destruction on southern Sudan—appeared to be for adolescent women.

On her travels, Meiram even encountered liberated slaves who warned her that the only way she could get herself freed would be if a relative came and reclaimed her—and then that would require a bribe to the local police.

Poor Meiram did not have a single living relative. Her situation seemed doomed. Even the tears she used to shed every night after letting those three masters have sex with her had disappeared. Her emotions were being wrung dry by the hopelessness of her situation.

She felt thoroughly used, abused, and discarded. She no longer trusted anyone in the world. The three men who would take it in turns to sleep with her had almost become, in a twisted way, her only protectors.

For the first few months of her ''marriage'' to the threesome, they'd often handcuffed her at night to stop her trying to escape and to make it easier to force themselves upon her.

But soon the men mistook her resigned acceptance as a sign of compliance and they stopped keeping her manacled at night. To begin with, this newfound freedom did not provoke a flutter of a response from the muted young slave girl.

The evenings had taken on a repetitive mold all of their own. As night fell, Meiram would be given a bowl of food to build up her strength for the coming sexual activities, and sometimes even a glass of illicit home-brewed alcohol to win her over. Then Mahmoud would always be the first to start fumbling with her. And so it went.

But on one particular evening when the third of her masters crawled on top of her as she lay there resigned to her fate, she got a nasty surprise. For he had brought a friend along and insisted that she should also have sex with him.

Meiram was outraged by the suggestion. Her protestations were naturally ignored but the indignity of having a complete stranger introduced to the proceedings suddenly awoke the spirit within her.

"How dare they treat me like this!" she decided. How could she have just lain there for all those months and done nothing?

Meiram was more angry with herself than anyone else. She started to tense up when the stranger mounted her, then she relaxed. She decided there and then to make her escape that night and she did not intend to give them any excuse to ever put her back in shackles again.

That night, Meiram waited until she was sure all four men were fast asleep in their tents. She even counted the snores and the snorts to be absolutely sure because she knew that this might be her only chance.

Her incarceration was based on the fact she had nowhere else to run and therefore would never dare escape from their clutches.

But they had not counted on her cunning.

Meiram silently gathered up her few belonging and headed off for the outskirts of the small town where they were staying at the time.

"I had no idea where we were but I knew I just had to keep heading north, where it was safer," she says.

Meiram took immediate advantage of the deep, moonless night and let the stars guide her as far north of the town as she could get before dawn.

Then, as the sun rose, she climbed the nearest bushy tree to hide until the sun set.

"It was the only way I stood a chance," she explained.

The first two days on the run were definitely the most risky because Meiram feared that every person she passed might be heading into that same town and would tell her masters they had seen her heading north.

On the second day, Meiram was hiding in a tall tree when she heard two men talking below her and she became convinced they were looking for her. She

never knew for sure whether that was her own un-
derstandable built-in paranoia but she became even
more cautious during her journey the following night.

After six hard days of travelling, she reached a rel-
atively friendly outpost that had remained virtually
unaffected by the war. The first person she met was
a woman who was looking for a housekeeper to look
after her baby. Meiram, who had once had baby sisters of her own, leapt at the chance and thanked her
lucky stars for being alive. Maybe life was worth living after all.

Enslavement in the Sudan region has much religious
underpinning. Many of the Dinka people are Chris-
tians; only a few are Muslim. Government radio
broadcasts at the time actually endorsed the military
raids as a "*jihad* against the pagans." Among the
Misseriya, the word *abide* or "slave," has been used
to refer not only to domestic slaves but also to those
who, because they were non-Muslims, could have
been appropriately captured and turned into slaves.

As one human rights activist in the Sudan commented, "If the governments of the U.S. and Britain
have normal relations with the government of Sudan;
they are condoning slavery."

With Western governments still attaching low priority to human rights issues in the Sudan, many observers fear that the residents of the south of the
country will continue to pay a heavy price.

10

WAGES OF FEAR

Machines are worshipped because they are beautiful, and valued because they confer power; they are hated because they are hideous, and loathed because they impose slavery.
Bertrand Russell (1928)

MARINA DRIVE, QUINCY, NEAR BOSTON, AUGUST 28, 1992

"You will not walk alone outside the apartment."

"Why not?" Vasantha Gedara asked her new employer.

"Because the police will kill you or a stranger will rape you."

"Oh."

Perhaps Vasantha should have taken heed of that lecture and realized it was a severe warning of the problems that were to follow, but then she was a 22-year-old woman in desperate need of a job and Kuwaiti Talal Alzanki seemed a responsible type of person. She had even worked for his mother back in the Middle East.

He was a 30-year-old Boston University electrical engineering graduate with a pregnant 21-year-old wife whom he seemed to genuinely love and adore.

Sri Lankan maid Vasantha was fully aware that Kuwaitis were not always the easiest people in the world to work for, but she was now in the United States of America, so it couldn't possibly end up like some of those horror stories she had come across in the Middle East.

Little did she realize that the journey she had just taken from Boston's Logan International Airport was the last time she would be allowed outdoors for four months.

When Alzanki showed Vasantha to her room she was in for yet another surprise. There was no bed, not even a mattress, and her "room" was actually a corner of the hallway.

Alzanki explained calmly yet coldly, "You are not permitted to sit on the furniture."

"But I cannot sleep without a mattress."

"Too bad."

Something about his attitude told Vasantha not to argue with Alzanki that day. She needed the job badly and, hopefully, her new employers would mellow as time passed. She did not even object when he insisted that she hand over her money and passport "for safe-keeping" the moment she entered the apartment.

The first few days in the Alzanki apartment in the Boston suburb of Quincy were very quiet. Neither husband nor wife seemed to say much to each other, and Mrs. Alzanki was forbidden from talking to her maid.

Vasantha, 28, tried to get on with the jobs Mr. Alzanki had ordered her to perform when she first went for the interview for the job.

Alzanki tended to work long hours at the university and his strictly Muslim wife was not permitted to leave the apartment unless accompanied by her husband.

One of the first big mistakes that Vasantha made was to be caught sitting down on a kitchen chair when the master of the house came back from the university.

Without any pleasantries, Alzanki steamed right in. "Get off that chair. I told you not to use any of the furniture. If you disobey me again, you will die!"

Vasantha was petrified by this threat but decided that since he had asked her not to use the furniture when she started, she would concede to him this once.

She scuttled off to her bare, miniscule living area off the kitchen and tried to bury herself in a book.

Suddenly, she heard Alzanki shouting and screaming at the top of his voice. He was speaking Arabic to his wife, but she could tell it was not a polite conversation. There was an angry exchange of words going on.

Just as quickly the proceedings snapped back to complete silence. Vasantha thought nothing more about it until she suddenly heard a loud crash and a scream from Mrs. Alzanki.

She rushed out of her corner of the hall and was

going through the kitchen towards the sitting room area when Alzanki came charging through towards her.

"Get back in your room. Now!"

Vasantha turned around, convinced that he was about to hit her next, unless she did as she was told.

The following 111 days at that Quincy apartment turned into a nightmare of human degradation and enslavement.

After about two weeks, Vasantha "dared" to inquire about when her promised wages would start being paid.

"You will be paid when I decide to pay you," came the reply.

She was not allowed to make any phone calls and was forbidden from looking out of the window or stepping outside.

When Thanksgiving weekend occurred in November, 1992, the Alzankis announced they were going upstate to visit some friends and Vasantha was "not to leave the apartment under any circumstances."

"There's pita bread and some fresh water in the refrigerator," barked Alzanki in his regulation tone. That was all she had *ever* been offered to eat.

Vasantha looked aghast. He noticed her expression and added his own little afterword.

"If you leave the apartment I will know . . . and remember what I told you about the police. They will shoot a single woman out at night in this neighborhood."

* * *

When the Alzankis returned from their Thanksgiving weekend, things went from bad to worse.

The master of the house insisted that Vasantha use a particularly noxious cleaning chemical to scour the entire apartment from top to bottom. The liquid was almost like pure acid, and rapidly the Sri Lankan slave girl's eyes were running profusely and she was in a lot of pain.

About two-thirds of the way through her cleaning duties she fainted and cut her head on a table leg as she fell. The Alzankis refused her request to call a doctor when she recovered consciousness.

By the late fall of 1992, the couple completely banned Vasantha from mailing any letters to her family back home.

Mr. Alzanki also reminded Vasantha that because her job with them had been arranged through a Kuwaiti employment agency, they were perfectly within their rights to put her on a plane back to the Middle East if she did not perform her duties satisfactorily.

With this threat ringing in her ears and a constant fear of returning to Kuwait, Vasantha felt obliged to continue to struggle on for this couple from hell.

Throughout most of this Mrs. Alzanki had remained fairly quiet and reserved, and Vasantha even presumed that her reluctance to speak was caused by a scant knowledge of English. She could not have been more wrong.

On December 17, 1992, Mrs. Alzanki became incredibly angry with her slave girl after she accidently dropped a plate on the kitchen floor.

"Next time, I will sew your mouth shut and kill you," she screamed at her servant.

Not surprisingly, Vasantha was terrified.

On the actual domestic front, work at the Alzanki apartment was taking on monumental proportions.

Vasantha was now cleaning the bathroom at least four times a day and replacing shelf paper in kitchen cupboards daily. She was also forced to clean the carpet with a whisk broom and wash clothes and dishes by hand, even though machines were available.

She was even denied dental treatment for an abscessed tooth, which eventually fell out.

Her original paltry wage of $4.50 a day had still not materialized.

After the birth of the Alzankis' son, life inside the apartment became slightly easier, if only because of the two friendly nurses who worked shifts looking after the infant.

Both of them were horrified by the way that the Alzankis were treating Vasantha. One of them commented, "They're treating you like an animal. It's disgraceful."

Eventually, the two nurses hatched a plan to get Vasantha safely out of the apartment and into the nearest police station to report the full story of her horrific experiences.

"You've either got to go to the police or your local consul. Someone has to be told what these people are doing to you."

For the following few weeks, the scheme was carefully thought through as the two nurses smuggled in proper food for Vasantha and contacted a friendly policeman to take on the case.

The Alzankis were arrested by FBI agents on slavery charges for allegedly forcing Vasantha to work against her will, while paying her little and depriving her of food. They were also charged with conspiracy and involuntary servitude in a federal indictment that detailed a long list of abuses against Vasantha Gedara over the four-month period she worked for them.

She was in the country legally while working for the Alzankis, but became an illegal immigrant after leaving their home. She then applied for political asylum and received a work authorization permit. The Alzankis, it emerged, were in the U.S. on a student visa.

Shortly after their arrest, Theodore Merritt and Steven M. Dettelbach, a civil rights attorney with the justice department, urged a magistrate to hold Talal Alzanki without bail until trial.

In a chaotic scene, Mrs. Alzanki started sobbing uncontrollably when U.S. Magistrate-Judge Lawrence P. Cohen ordered him detained until a detention hearing at noon the next day. Mrs. Alzanki was to be confined to her apartment under house arrest. Prosecutors were told that her culture prohibited her from being separated from her husband and that she must return to Kuwait if he was jailed.

"It is going to be very difficult for me to take care

of myself without Talal,'' she sobbed to the court. ''I can't live without Talal. How will I support myself? Since he hasn't been proved guilty, why do you want to incarcerate him today?'' she implored.

To make matters worse, Mrs. Alzanki did not drive and could not, under Kuwait custom, be driven home by a strange man.

Prosecutors called it ''a case of modern-day slavery enforced by fear.'' Defense lawyers contended that Vasantha had always been free to leave and that she was just a lonely maid stuck in a bad job.

In May, 1994, Alzanki was found guilty of enslaving Vasantha and ordered to serve one year and a day in prison for involuntary servitude and pay the woman $13,400 in back wages.

Alzanki had been in line for an 18- to 24-month term under federal sentencing guidelines, but U.S. District Judge Rya Zobel said she considered the hardship Alzanki's imprisonment would impose on his wife, who had given birth to another child by the time the case came to trial.

Earlier, Alzanki himself had insisted that he was fully satisfied with Vasantha's work and her cooking and that she had overreacted to his rules.

However, jurist Patricia Hurley said of Alzanki's testimony, ''We didn't believe a word he said.''

The case against Mrs. Alzanki had ended in a mistrial the previous week, after she gave birth to the new baby.

U.S. Attorney Donald K. Stern said, ''The jury's verdict makes clear that the most vulnerable of people deserve no less than our vigorous efforts.''

And Vasantha's lawyer, Sarah Burgess Reed, said her client was elated by the verdict. She has now gotten herself a job working as a nanny for an American family in Massachusetts.

11

SISTERS OF TERROR

*Freedom is indivisible, and when one man is
enslaved, all are not free.*
John F. Kennedy (1963)

Princesses Simiya and Faria al-Sabah, half-sisters of
the Emir of Kuwait, were considered strangely exotic
creatures on London's West End nightclub circuit.

Their designer dresses and almost daily hairstyling
and manicure sessions, along with a mass of gold jewelry on both wrists, their necks, and virtually every
finger, gave the distinct impression they were very,
very wealthy—and not afraid to show it.

But beneath the glitter and glamour lay the minds
of two evil sadists who spent part of every day for
four years severely punishing their own personal slave
girl to within an inch of her life.

Laxmi Peria Swami still does not know her own
age, and her dark face and the black circles under her

eyes make it difficult to guess, but she is probably approaching 50 now. The two princesses refused to tell her how old she was. They preferred to taunt and punish her. They loved to make her feel as if she had no right to any life outside the four walls of their luxurious London home.

This particular day had started just like any other for Laxmi during her employment in that appalling household.

The two princesses had stayed in bed until around midday after yet another night on the town, something they could never have dared do back in their native Kuwait.

Simiya and Faria hardly had time to adjust their eyes to the midday sun, when they decided it was time for Laxmi to earn her keep.

They didn't once take into consideration that Laxmi had been standing and waiting for them throughout the time they were out nightclubbing the previous evening, as was her duty. She had to do that every time her mistresses went out.

"Stand on this spot and do not move until we return," Faria told her slave girl when they first began going out until the early hours after arriving in London from Kuwait.

By the time Laxmi got to her tiny cubbyhole by the kitchen, it would be entirely fair to say that she was probably even more exhausted than the two spoiled Arab princesses. And all she got to live on was a strip of cold wood floor in a passageway by the kitchen, with a two-inch mattress and little else in the way of home comforts.

"I need a massage," hissed Simiya at Laxmi as the mistress stretched her arms in the midday sun, which was peeping through a slight gap in the silky curtains of her interior-designed bedroom. Her sister turned over and slipped back into a light slumber on the bed next to her.

Laxmi took a deep breath, let the air slowly out of her nose and pulled up the sleeves of her cheap cotton smock.

"Wash your hands first. I don't know where they've been."

Laxmi did not reply but walked toward the bathroom. She had long since learned that she should never talk back to the sisters unless they asked her a specific question.

"Not in there, you idiot. In the kitchen," muttered Simiya contemptuously.

By the time Laxmi returned a few minutes later, Simiya was lying on the soft mattress gossiping to a girlfriend on the phone. She did not even look up when Laxmi appeared by her side.

Instead, Simiya rolled over on her stomach, spread her legs slightly and just lay there in her pink satin nightgown waiting to be pampered.

"Oh, this guy was so beautiful. I could've eaten him on the spot," she giggled to her friend on the phone. "His eyes were so blue . . ."

"*Come on!*"

Laxmi rolled up the long satin nightdress so that it

exposed the cellulite-swamped thighs of her mistress. A slightly unpleasant aroma wafted through the air, but it was nothing compared with what she had experienced since arriving in London with the princesses.

"So," she continued to her girlfriend. "I played it really cool with him, you know. Hold on a minute." Simiya turned and looked up at Laxmi. "Harder. Do it harder!"

Laxmi did as her mistress commanded.

"Not that fucking hard."

She eased off, well aware that she had momentarily allowed herself to think and act beyond her station.

Outside the house, on the busy, civilized streets of Mayfair, the rich and beautiful were shopping in the swank stores of Piccadilly unaware that a poor, innocent, illiterate slave girl was being bullied and cajoled in a life that was more miserable than the most Dickensian of nightmares.

As Simiya continued babbling on the phone like some adolescent schoolgirl, Laxmi allowed her mind to drift back to the days when she was a poverty-stricken but happy young woman with her four young children on the streets of Delhi.

Here she was, trapped in a palace of misery thousands of miles from her offspring, whom she had been prevented from contacting for the best part of four years. Laxmi did not even know her children's location. Occasionally one of the older ones would write to her and if she was lucky the princesses would read the letters to her. But she had no actual address for them.

Suddenly, the slave girl was snapped out of her daydreaming trance by the crunching pain of a stiletto heel smashing into her shin. It was Faria.

"Put more into it," she spat at Laxmi.

On the bed, Simiya was still talking to her girl-friend on the phone, but a sneering smile came to her lips when she saw her sister kicking their slave girl.

Laxmi tried her hardest to respond to her orders, but she was clearly exhausted. Unfortunately, her weary expression simply added fuel to the fire of rage within the two evil royal sisters.

"I said, do it harder," yelled Faria at their servant.

As Laxmi increased the pressure with her hands sinking into the folds of the flesh of the backs of her mistress's chubby thighs, Simiya sighed. It could have been a sign of pleasure or perhaps just the pure satisfaction of knowing that you are in complete and utter control of another human being. Whatever the case, those two sisters were on the ultimate kick. They owned every inch of Laxmi, and they would never let her forget it.

Laxmi tried not to think about the possible sexual implications of many of her duties for the princesses. She did not question many of their requests for the sort of massages that seemed to have little to do with aching bones and more to do with orgasmic pleasure.

Just then, Simiya turned over onto her back and instructed Laxmi to pull up her nightgown entirely. Neither of the sisters had any inhibitions about their bodies in front of their slave girl. They considered Laxmi to be a subhuman being so her emotions and feelings never once came into the equation. She was expected to wash every inch of their bodies by hand and do precisely the same when massaging them.

Faria sat down on the lush bedroom armchair and examined her perfectly manicured pink fingernails as Laxmi continued to body massage her sister.

"Hurry up, we need to be at that restaurant opposite Harrods by one," she commented matter-of-factly.

Laxmi wondered to herself why on earth Faria had kicked her as she massaged her sister. She thought perhaps it was a show of strength on the part of the older sister. Faria did it to her virtually every time she was attending to Simiya. She also noticed that Faria was nearly always fully dressed when she lashed out. Those black patent stilettos or some other similar such pair of shoes would always be the first point of pain. Laxmi had never dared asked her why she was being beaten. It had just become a habit.

"She's so pathetic. Look at her." Faria did not even bother looking up from her nails as she started to castigate her slave girl.

Just then, she eased up her pencil skirt, exposing at least three inches of thigh, and pulled her leg back before aiming her spiky heel directly at Laxmi's backside.

Faria laughed.

"There's certainly not much to sink my toes into."

*   *   *

Twenty minutes later, Faria and Simiya were just about to depart when they decided to bark some last-minute orders at their slave girl Laxmi.

"You won't have time for lunch," Faria said coldly.

Then Simiya chipped in, "Make sure you throw away all the remains from dinner last night." As an afterthought, she added, "Pour some drink over it and then put it straight in the dustbins outside."

That was the cruelest order of all. It was even worse than the sadistic beatings as far as Laxmi was concerned, for it meant that she could not eat any of the remains of the Harrods-delivered cuisine that had been half-wasted by the eight guests who'd been round at the house for lunch the previous day.

Sometimes Laxmi would be so hungry that she would stretch through the kitchen window to grab something from the dustbins to satisfy her under-standable craving for some real food.

The only liquid Laxmi was ever allowed was water from the tap in the tiny maid's bathroom next to that cold passageway by the kitchen. Most nights, Laxmi would curl up on that paper-thin mattress hours after the princesses had gone to bed, having ensured the entire house was spotlessly clean so that they would not attack her the moment they woke the next morn-ing.

Laxmi could not remember a night when she had not cried herself to sleep since arriving in London. Her dreams were the only escape from the pain and anguish of reality. She would find herself back in India, with the children in the middle of the countryside, smiling faces, happy, contented. But then something dreadful would happen and those dreams would turn into horrendous nightmares that usually awoke Laxmi with a terrible start and snapped her cruelly back into the reality of her awful situation.

A few hours later, Laxmi would find herself standing in front of those two evil mistresses awaiting her first punishment of the day, which usually consisted of a punch in the stomach or a kick in the kidneys if she was even a few seconds late in waking them up.

Although Laxmi was never actually shackled, she felt an enormous psychological pressure not to even contemplate leaving the princesses. They would frequently warn her that if she ever ran away, the Kuwaiti secret police would track her down and kill her. Laxmi had no reason to disbelieve them and it terrified her. She convinced herself that it was her fate to stay trapped in that house of horrors for the rest of her life.

At least when the princesses read her children's letters they seemed to be showing some compassion towards her. But Laxmi did not realize that those letters simply represented another piece of twisted, sadistic behavior on the part of her mistresses.

For both of them had taken to making up entire sections of the letters just to tease and taunt their slave girl and ensure that she would never leave their employment.

One time, they told her that her beloved son had been killed in a motor-bike accident. It was a cruel hoax on the part of the sisters, but Laxmi wasn't to know that. She burst into tears as soon as they started telling her about the "tragedy."

The sisters' response was predictably brutal.

"Shut up," they sneered.

But for once Laxmi could not obey their command. She was so distraught by the news that she became even more hysterical.

Faria walked over towards her. Perhaps she was going to break the habit of a lifetime and show some compassion?

The rings on her fingers made the first backhanded slap particularly painful for Laxmi. The three or four hits that followed were numbed by the slave girl's deeply emotional state.

When she had finished, Faria turned to Simiya.

"It's your turn."

Simiya giggled childishly and stood up. She must have just caught the snap of fear in Laxmi's eyes as she clenched her fist for the first punch.

Eventually, Laxmi stopped crying but the tears inside her would never dry up. She suffered the beating in just the same way she had suffered everything over the previous four years—with complete numbness. She had become so used to being abused that she had stopped wondering why it was happening. She never once noticed the smiles of satisfaction on the faces of her two mistresses as they tried to beat the spirit out of their slave girl forever.

It wasn't until many years later that Laxmi discovered her son had not died.

And Laxmi wasn't the only slave girl working for the brutal princesses. The other servant in the household, a Sri Lankan called Shamsu, was forced to place her hand directly on to an electric ring on the cooker and was badly burned.

The princesses were about to make Laxmi do the same, but one of them pointed out, "If we do that, we won't have anyone left to do the housework."

Laxmi was particularly haunted by one awful incident that had happened when she first started working for the princesses in Kuwait before they began the regular trips to their luxurious home in London.

She was taken to see three men who were being publicly hanged and both the princesses told her, "If you do anything wrong, this is what will happen to you." Laxmi never doubted their word.

In fact, throughout her employment with the princesses, her tiny wages had been withheld even though they were supposed to send them on to her family in India. Laxmi never received one penny from her two mistresses during her employment with them.

The princesses treated Laxmi and Shamsu like luggage as they accompanied the royal party back and forth to London, where the two mistresses were free from the strict religious restrictions imposed on them in Kuwait.

After one particularly brutal incident during which both of the princesses turned on Laxmi and tried to strangle her, Laxmi managed to escape from the house when the front door, which was usually locked, was accidently left open.

The slave girl ran into the street, crying and bleeding, and a passing taxi took her to the Indian High Commission, which then sent her back to the princesses because she did not have any money to pay for her airfare back to India.

After that abortive escape attempt the princesses began punishing Laxmi on an even more regular basis. They also denied her all freedom of movement; doors and windows to the house were barred from the outside. The princesses established complete and utter dominance over Laxmi, ensuring her absolute obedience.

Laxmi continued to sleep in the passageway outside the kitchen, but now it was always locked. She was not allowed any clothes of her own and she was given nothing other than the occasional scrap of bread.

Whenever she was caught taking food from the dustbin through the barred window she would be beaten by either or both of the princesses. Initially, they used a broomstick, but then one day Faria appeared in the kitchen brandishing a horsewhip and started lashing out at Laxmi's bottom.

"You will only eat when we tell you. Do you understand?"

Laxmi nodded weakly.

"Now bend over."

The numbness of receiving regular punishments had been replaced by a complete and utter emptiness.

There was no life beyond this hellish existence—or so it seemed.

Sometimes the princesses would come back from riding in Hyde Park and find some excuse or other to punish Laxmi, although it seemed more likely that they were getting some sort of thrill out of whipping their slave girl while dressed in jodhpurs and black leather boots.

Occasionally, the princesses would use knotted electrical cords just to vary the form of punishments they meted out. By this time, slave girls Laxmi and Shamsu were banned from talking to each other, and if they were ever spotted in conversation they could take it for granted that a severe beating would follow.

But probably the worse incident of all occured when the princesses accused Laxmi of not cleaning the house properly.

''You're filthy. You stink. You're pathetic,'' they taunted their slave girl.

Then one of the princesses started squinting at Laxmi.

''I want that gold in your mouth.''

Laxmi did not reply. She feared she knew what was coming next.

The princesses then produced a huge pair of pliers. One of them held her down and the other started some dental removal work. Somehow, the screams that filled the house that evening escaped the attention of any of the princesses' neighbors.

*   *   *

Eventually, the other servant, Shamsu, escaped from the house with the help of a local Indian from whom she had begged for scraps of food when she was starving. He felt sorry for her and told her to go to the Sri Lankan High Commission. There, for the first time, the full story of the horrific regime under the two satanic princesses was revealed.

Sri Lankan officials alerted the police to the plight of Laxmi, who was still living in the house.

When a group of policemen from Paddington Green station, led by Detective Sergeant Steve Gaskin, entered the princesses' house with a search warrant to rescue her, Laxmi was terrified and at first refused to go with them. She thought they had come on the princesses' orders to hang her.

The police eventually persuaded her to leave with them and they took her to a refuge in Brent, North West London, where she began to receive counselling for the horrendous years she had spent in captivity.

One of the first things the police did was ask a doctor to examine Laxmi. He found 97 scars on her body, some of which, he said, would never heal. Her eyes had been damaged when one of the princesses had thrown a set of keys into her face.

Laxmi was also seen by an ophthalmologist, a dentist—who found clear evidence of the removal of those two gold teeth—and a psychiatrist—all of whose evidence was to prove crucial in the years ahead. Their findings substantiated her claims when they finally reached the civil courts five years later.

Long before that, criminal proceedings were initiated, but the two princesses denied the main charges of grievous bodily harm, actual bodily harm, and conspiracy to cause bodily harm. By the time the case came to Knightsbridge Crown Court in 1985, many of these charges had been dropped. Some suspected that was a direct attempt to placate the Kuwaiti government. The princesses were eventually given six-month suspended sentences and Laxmi was awarded compensation: $400 on one count and $2,300 for another—sums which, to princesses from one of the richest families in the world, were small change.

Laxmi was livid that they had got off with such light punishments and sought fresh legal advice to start civil legal proceedings against her onetime mistresses. Then followed six years of hard work, many setbacks, and a case of astonishing complexity.

Laxmi's lawyer Rohit Sanghvi began work on her case by looking back through more than a century of cases, searching for precedents. There were none. No servant in Britain had ever brought a successful action against an employer for unlawful imprisonment and grievous bodily harm.

In the case of the Kuwaiti princesses there was another problem: finding them. Laxmi could not supply an address in Kuwait, and they also owned homes elsewhere. The police needed an address in order to serve the civil warrant.

There were problems for Laxmi too. Her allegations had to be substantiated. She had undergone a series of physical examinations for medical reports; not only by experts from her own side, but experts for her employers too, seeking to undermine her claims. For a deeply modest, nervous woman these examinations were an ordeal.

The tactics of the princesses and their lawyers were simply to try and wear Laxmi down; to destroy her ability to go through with the case. At every possible stage of the legal proceedings they were obstructive. Until just before the civil case was due to be heard, they denied all charges—even those to which they had already pleaded guilty in the criminal court. They even claimed that the two servants had beaten each other.

Finally, the princesses realized that even they, members of one of the richest and most powerful dynasties in the Middle East, were not immune to the persistence of a dedicated lawyer and an unshakable witness who will bear the evidence on her own body for the rest of her life.

For her pain and suffering at the time, and for her continued suffering afterward, for her nightmares, terrors, traumas, and unlawful imprisonment, Laxmi was awarded $500,000 by a High Court jury on December 8, 1989. To this was added a further $30,000 in interest to cover the delays. Legal aid costs of about $150,000 were awarded against the princesses, whose own legal bill amounted to at least three times as much.

It will come as no surprise to learn that it took a further year to get the money out of the princesses. Ironically, if it had not been for Iraq's invasion of

Kuwait, and the country's need for Western support, it might never have been paid.

As for Laxmi, she does not doubt that it was all worthwhile.

"After the long struggle I feel I was entitled to what I got as recompense for all my pain. To them, the money is nothing, it's like air; but it's my body they abused, and every scar on my body reminds me of what I went through. No amount of money was worth that.

"What matters to me is that the truth of my story has been recognized; that I was believed by the judge and jury—that was what mattered. It was a vindication that I was believed and not the princesses. I could have just died in this country, and nobody would have known or cared. And for all we know, many others do die."

12

INNOCENCE FOR SALE

This is a world of compensation; and he who would be no slave must consent to have no slave. Those who deny freedom to others deserve it not for themselves, and, under a just God, cannot long retain it.
    Abraham Lincoln (1859)

WOTGANJ MARKET, CALCUTTA, INDIA, AUGUST, 1992

A group of girls barely out of their teens played noisily by a gushing fire hydrant, their shrieks of laughter echoing round the squalid side street as thousands of people hummed through this incredibly busy thoroughfare.

One girl, dressed head to toe in white cotton with two jet-black braids of hair tumbling down the front of her shoulders, stood out from the rest of the children in the middle of their game.

Saida was just thirteen years old, yet had the demeanor of someone in her late teens, even early twenties. More than half a dozen bracelets dangled from her bony wrists. On her feet, neat gold sandals entrapped her carefully painted toenails.

Suddenly an older woman called Anwari standing by an abandoned shopfront, beckoned the child over towards her. Saida moved dutifully away from her friends. None of them seemed to notice or care as she broke away and strode purposefully toward that older woman.

"All the young ones are virgins, we can guarantee that. The older ones will not be, they will have done some work," commented Anwari to the man standing next to her on the edge of that busy marketplace.

These are the mean streets of Calcutta and anything goes if a man requires it. On this occasion, a well-dressed Arab was seeking an unblemished sexual partner, possibly as his wife.

He turned to "Godmother" Anwari while young Saida was still making her way toward them.

"How do you know she is a virgin?"

"We know," came the terse reply.

This is the ultimate human supermarket where people are sold like any other goods. They even have a choice of nationalities available—Chinese, Bangladeshi, Assamese, Tibetan and, of course, Indian. They are aged from 10 upward.

"Do you like what you see?" weary Anwari asked her prospective client as the young Saida got closer.

"Hmmm. Yes. She looks perfect. How much?"

"Three thousand," snapped back Anwari, safe in the knowledge that she had paid $100 to their parents for the right to sell their children off at the market.

"Too much. I'll give you $1,500."

"No way. Forget it."

Just then Saida came alongside her "godmother" and the man who planned to bed her within hours, and then turn her into his own personal bride/sex slave.

"Show the gentleman your teeth, my dear."

Saida bared her white, gleaming ivories.

"Very good," said the Arab without a twitch of discomfort.

This strange threesome then walked off toward the labyrinth of side streets to finalize negotiations away from any spying policemen not bribable enough to ignore the sale of yet another human being at Watganj Market.

Eventually, Anwari succeeded in haggling the price up to $2,600, which represented a very healthy profit on an initial outlay of no more than $100. The human slave trade is still very much alive and well in many of the most famous cities in the world.

A few hours later, poor innocent Saida was being subjected to the horrendous experience of losing her virginity at an age when most little girls are playing with dolls.

In some ways, though, she turned out to be one of the luckier ones. Her master was not as brutal as many of the men who purchase their own sex slaves with alarming regularity in this seedy, depressing market.

At least she was not handcuffed to a bed each night

to prevent her from escaping. At least she was being well fed. At least he was paying for her to buy some new clothes.

But the fact remains that Saida was yet another innocent lost.

No one keeps actual records of such unsavory transactions but it is estimated that more than half of these child bride/slaves will die before they reach the grand old age of 40. Abuse by their master/husband is the most common cause of death. However, many are just abandoned in the streets after a handful of years of sexual and physical abuse because it is so easy for men to find themselves replacement slaves.

In Saida's case, her apparently ''reasonable'' master will probably turn abusive eventually, and then she will be lucky if she gets out alive.

''But what choice is there here for a young person?'' says one local child welfare expert. ''They have little chance of a job. To some, the life of a slave/wife is far preferable to starving on the streets.''

Back on the streets near the chaotic market of Watganj, the talk is mostly of money.

''You want a virgin. I got just the girl,'' insists a small Indian called Denis, who looks and behaves a lot like Dustin Hoffman in *Midnight Cowboy*. This guy is greasy, sweaty, and smelly.

Suddenly other hustlers appear alongside any prospective buyers. They sense that a deal is going down, and they want a chance to offer an ever better bargain.

''You want girl to keep? No problem.''

"Best girls. All virgins."

"Young and clean. The only way."

And so it goes on.

Meanwhile, dozens of other beady eyes lock onto anyone with apparent wealth.

The attraction of child bride/slaves is obvious. This is a country where most people earn about $5 a week. The chance to make a thumping profit will always take priority.

The slave girl network in Calcutta is a carefully orchestrated industry. Loose tongues can wreck the business overnight. It is an organized crime network where protection is absolutely essential.

Godmothers like Anwari have at least two armed guards close by at all times making sure that no one tries to rip her off or inform on her to the police.

Often she finalizes negotiations at the nearby Victorian Memorial Gardens, a clear open space with plenty of people wandering around.

Anwari soon forgot her "godchild" Saida, who was now gone off with the Arab to her new life. Her latest concern was another customer whom she met earlier that day. She arranged to let him inspect more than a dozen prospective slave girls at the park.

This is when the true horror of this terrible business really hits home. Most of them are just innocent children with not a clue about the horrors that await them in the outside world.

Their fate is quite simple. Like Saida they will

probably be married to their suitor within hours of meeting him.

Then, most probably, they'll be put on a boat and shipped out of India rather than attracting too much attention at the airport.

In 1991, a particularly horrendous case was exposed when a 61-year-old Arab was arrested at Delhi airport taking an 11-year-old girl home to the Middle East.

But the worst of it will occur when these innocent slave girls get to their final destinations. They will be sexually attacked, raped and brutalized, and when they are finished with them, they will either be put to work scrubbing floors or divorced and thrown out. Many will simply "disappear."

Anwari has a voice as cold as ice. She has been nurturing these innocents and their families since they were toddlers.

"They are healthy, beautiful creatures. Perfect for any man," says Anwari.

Now they're old enough, she has even bought them fine saris so they look their best to be sold off. Those who are not "lucky" enough to find a buyer will end up in a brothel.

Given the poverty of India, not to mention neighboring Bangladesh, with few families able to afford the expensive dowries that daughters require if they're to be married off, there's a plentiful supply of little girls for evil women like Anwari.

She usually buys the little girls from their parents,

who believe that their loved ones will be well cared for. Many of them are purchased for absolutely no charge. Small wonder it is such a profitable business.

The girls themselves remain blissfully unaware of their final destination in life. Their emotions have been, in many cases, virtually neutralized by years of non-parenting. They really have been bred to sell, just like cattle.

Meanwhile the more perceptive of them are resigned to their fate. After all, they've had hard lives already, earning their keep by cleaning the brothels and cooking for the older prostitutes of the houses where they live.

"None of the girls can read or write," says Anwari without any note of surprise in her voice. "They are all clean and virgins. I will guarantee that. They have never been touched by a man."

Anwari even asks the girls in front of prospective clients if they are virgins. They always nod their heads furiously.

Anwari even assures customers that "I have all the necessary paperwork and can take care of everything including the marriage."

Three-quarters of her fee, she explains to her male clients, is payable before the "marriage" has taken place and the remainder is due straight afterwards.

"I will not take any less money because they have many years ahead of them to work in the brothels and that earns much money."

Anwari discusses the details of this disturbing transaction in much the same way she would conduct the sale of anything. She could be selling chappatis or trinkets in the market. It just happens to be the lives of some little girls in this case.

The girls themselves find it difficult to relate to the fact that they might be about to be shipped out to a foreign country. It is confusing. Up until this point most of their life has been spent working as maids in a row of brothels in a market. The idea of travelling thousands of miles must be bewildering.

Some of them often inquire about coming home to see their friends. Anwari answers them immediately. "Of course you will." In her mind it is far preferable to deceive the girls than tell them the truth.

"It's better that way," Anwari insists.

On this particular occasion in the wide open, safe space of the memorial park, Anwari's male client was uncertain which one of the girls wanted so none of them was chosen. The girls went back to the playground and started teasing one another like real children once again. Two pimps watching the entire proceedings dispersed and eventually marched over toward the play area.

The young girls immediately finished their game and start to follow their keepers, too young, too innocent and trusting to know of the fate that eventually awaits them . . .

13

JACKIE WHO?

*Slaves lose everything in their chains, even the
desire of escaping from them.*
Rousseau, *The Social Contract* (1762)

WALNUT GROVE, ROSEMEAD, CALIFORNIA, AUGUST, 1994

Neighbors in this suburban, tree-lined street, had for
some time been concerned by the activities at Number
2651, a two-story, stucco-fronted, wood-frame house
rented out by its owner to a stunningly attractive
Asian woman known only as Jackie.

Jackie never had a problem coming up with the
monthly rent of just over $1,000, so nobody really
had any right to object to her presence in the area.
But some of the longer-term residents of this classically suburban area near Los Angeles couldn't help
noticing the constant flow of cars that would pull up
in the driveway to the four-bedroom property.

''Jackie'' Suphonphan Wood, 29 years old, with a
propensity for designer-label outfits and weekly visits

to the beauty parlor was certainly a head-turner. She had the high cheekbones that often make Thai women classically beautiful, and she had the confidence of someone ten years older.

But then Jackie had every right to look like a rich, successful businesswoman because she was running a highly profitable industry importing female sex slaves from her home country. Her personal income was in excess of $200,000 a year.

Inside that immaculate residence were eight young Thai slave girls servicing up to 30 men a day between them. Their passports and money had been confiscated on arrival in California and they were paying off $30,000 "debts" by each having to sleep with upwards of 300 men.

Jackie made sure that there was a 24-hour guard at the house to prevent any of the girls escaping until their "debts" had been fully paid off. There was Jackie's boyfriend Tai Thahn Pham; Tom, a 20-year-old Vietnamese; and "security guard" Jimmy, another slightly older Vietnamese and various other men holding similar positions.

To make matters even worse, some of these men expected sex from the slave girls as part of their reward for keeping them prisoner in the house. One of the guards was particularly brutal and all the women complained to Jackie about how he forced them to have sex.

Jackie didn't really care. She wasn't paying the men vast salaries so her main priority was keeping them happy and if that meant allowing them to have free sex with the girls then so be it.

One such girl was pretty, petite, dark-haired Anuthida Nanthaphanit. Her story is a classic example of how the lure of America has continued to prove the downfall of so many innocent people.

Anuthida, 19, met a Thai man called "Luck" in an office where she worked in Bangkok.

"You could make a lot of money in America. A pretty girl like you," insisted Luck, a scrawny man in his late thirties.

"How?" asked innocent Anuthida.

"There are many good jobs in the States. I know many people there."

"Really?" Anuthida said, not realizing she was falling for the most obvious setup in the world.

"I know one woman who runs a very successful business, and she is always looking for new staff."

Anuthida couldn't believe her luck. The very thought of working in America filled her with excitement. To most Thai girls it was a dream that never came true. But then she remembered how she had heard it was extremely difficult to get work visas.

"No problem. This woman I know guarantees you the job and then they issue the work visa," Luck told her.

Luck had pulled the same line with so many girls that he could reel them in on automatic pilot. But this one was even easier than usual.

"Give me a photo of yourself, and I'll send it to

this woman. If she likes the look of you then we'll begin making the arrangements.''

''What arrangements?''

''Well, there's the airfare and the agency fee for arranging the job and work visa . . .''

Within a few weeks, Anuthida had scraped together $1,000, consisting of her own hard-earned savings and a huge loan from her family. It was a down payment to be paid back from her new job, but the long-term investment was obvious.

The plane trip across the Pacific was the first time Anuthida had ever been out of her own country. She felt incredibly nervous flying to a strange land, to strange people, to no real friends. But then she had to keep reminding herself of what a great opportunity this was. Her friends and family had told her that she had to make the best of it because this might be the only chance she ever got.

At Los Angeles International Airport, Anuthida was met by a Thai man who never even gave her his name, but he did drive a big Chevrolet. It was the largest car Anuthida had ever been inside in her life and its engine purred, unlike all those mopeds and tin heaps that filled the streets back home.

The man took Anuthida to a motel just a couple of miles from the airport where he said that the woman who was employing her would be meeting them. The man said little else during the journey, but Anuthida was too nervous to attach any significance to that. She was looking around in wonderment at the wide streets and huge houses that seemed to be everywhere.

Anuthida was a little thrown when she found a note from her new boss in the hotel room explaining that she could not get there until the next morning.

"You must stay here. She will collect you in the morning," was about all the man told her.

Anuthida had a sleepless night. A combination of jet lag and the fear of being alone in a foreign land had made her feel a tad nervous about the entire adventure. For the first time, she actually began to wonder whether it was all as straightforward as she had presumed.

That night, she tried to watch TV, but the extensive choice of channels was in a language she could not understand. In any case, she just could not concentrate. Every time there were any sounds near her room she got extremely scared.

At least twice, Anuthida heard people's voices in other rooms, and two men had a fight in the parking lot outside her door. Then, when she did finally get to sleep, an amorous couple in the next suite were having sex so noisily that the entire building seemed to shake.

Early next morning, there was a knock on the door.

"Hello, my name is Jackie," purred the attractive figure standing in front of Anuthida. She felt the woman's eyes pan up and down her body. "You're even prettier in the flesh."

Something about what Jackie said sent a shiver down Anuthida's spine. But she interpreted her reaction as being caused by a combination of exhaustion and the trepidation she felt at arriving in a new place.

However, any fears she might have had soon disappeared when she saw what an expensive car Jackie was driving.

"She must be extremely successful," thought poor, innocent Anuthida.

In the car, Jackie explained to her young recruit that her business was based in a quiet city called Rosemead, near Los Angeles.

"It's a very wealthy area. There is little or no crime, and the people are so civilized," gushed Jackie to the awed Anuthida.

As her car turned into the driveway of the house on Walnut Grove, the young Thai girl noticed a man hurrying out of the property and getting into a car that swiftly pulled away without even so much as acknowledging Jackie's arrival.

"Who was that?" asked Anuthida.

"Oh, that was a customer," replied Jackie coolly.

Anuthida was immediately struck by the strange smell when she stepped inside the house. It was a sickly-sweet aroma that wafted down the hallway from a number of rooms she could see at the end of a corridor.

"Come with me," beckoned Jackie. Anuthida followed her new boss out into the backyard of the house where the sun was baking hot, but at least that awful smell was not so apparent.

They sat at a garden table and Jackie opened up a file. Inside, Anuthida could see that same photograph she had provided to Luck all those months earlier in Bangkok.

"You're going to be a very successful girl for me," said Jackie.

Just then Anuthida noticed two skimpy Thai girls wandering through the house. An elderly man followed them through and grabbed one of the girls from behind. Then they disappeared down a corridor.

"I expect you to go with at least three men a day," said Jackie in a terribly matter-of-fact way.

"What?" replied Anuthida.

"Those are the terms if you are to repay the $30,000."

Anuthida was momentarily confused. Then she got her brain around the images she had absorbed in the previous few minutes. Girls. Men. Strange aromas. Money.

"This is a brothel?"

"What else d'you think it is?" snapped back Jackie.

Suddenly, a tall thin Vietnamese man called Tom appeared alongside Jackie.

"Take her inside and show her around," ordered Jackie.

"You can't make me do this. I'll go to the police."

"Do that and you're dead," came Jackie's icy response. Then she turned to Tom. "Take her. *Now!*"

Anuthida was grabbed by the arm and pushed towards the French doors leading into the house.

"Don't worry, my dear. You're a very pretty girl. All the men will want you and that debt will be paid off very quickly. You'll get $100 credit for each customer you serve.''

That afternoon, Anuthida was forced to have sex with an old Asian man of at least 70. He stank and was very rough. That night, she cried herself to sleep in a single bed that she was forced to share with one of the other slave girls called Phanthila. They hardly exchanged any conversation before bedding down together. Jackie had warned the girls not to talk to each other. The punishment for breaking that rule was a severe beating followed by painful sex with one of the guards.

The following morning the girls were awakened by Jackie at 6:30 A.M. and told to clean up the house in preparation for a busy day.

"We have at least a dozen customers booked in today. I want the place looking immaculate," barked Jackie.

Then she turned to Anuthida. "You're coming with me."

"Where?"

"Just get her in the car," Jackie told Tom.

Jackie drove with Tom sitting in the back of the car next to Anuthida just in case she tried to make a run for it.

"You would be foolish to try and leave us because we would find you," said Jackie to her newest sex slave recruit as they pulled up outside a rundown building in a predominantly Asian area some 10 miles from the house in Rosemead.

"What is this place?" asked Anuthida.

"You'll find out soon enough," snapped Jackie.

They walked up to a back door to the building and Jackie knocked three times. An Asian man answered the door, looked around and then showed them inside the property.

Jackie then pointed to a door. "Go in there and wait for the doctor."

"What?"

"Just do it."

Anuthida went into the room. It was small and musty with no window. There was a gurney in the corner and one tatty-looking table lamp on the wooden floor.

Just then a short, fat, balding Asian man walked in wearing a tea-stained white doctor's coat. From a bag he produced a syringe.

"What's going on?" asked a fearful Anuthida.

"Shut up, you whore."

"But what are you going to do to me?"

"We're going to make sure you don't start breeding," came the terse reply.

Within an hour, Anuthida had a Norplant birth control device implanted in her and was back in the car, returning to Rosemead. This time she did not say one word to Jackie. Her fate was sealed. She was resigned to working as a sex slave. She tried to hold back the tears, but it was impossible not to weep.

"Shut up," said Jackie. "You're in America, the land of opportunity." She laughed.

For the following four months, Anuthida was expected to sleep with clients at any time of the day or night that Jackie demanded.

The other girls who worked at the house with her all seemed to have given up any hope of ever staying on in California once their so-called debt to Jackie had been paid off. They all said they felt so battered by what had happened that they intended to return to Thailand as soon as they were released.

Unfortunately, Jackie had been entirely correct about one thing; Anuthida was immensely popular with the male customers because she was young and extremely attractive.

Two of the other slave girls were very nasty towards Anuthida because they believed she was deliberately trying to lure customers away from them in an effort to pay off her debt more quickly than anyone else. But the truth was that Anuthida's innocence and beauty were proving a fatal attraction to many of the customers.

Jackie was delighted by Anuthida's popularity because it meant that many men were using the services of her brothel more frequently than before.

Sometimes, Jackie would force Anuthida to go with her to a hotel to meet richer clients, many of whom were Korean businessman passing through California.

At first, Anuthida refused to go with Jackie to a hotel on the basis that she would not be able to protect herself in the event that the client expected to do something "too kinky."

Jackie was furious at Anuthida's defiance and got one of the bodyguards to handcuff her and march her into the back of her limo. It became clear to Anuthida that there was little point in resisting, even though she at no time accepted the fact that she was working as a prostitute.

In Anuthida's mind she was a sex slave to an evil woman and her brigade of bullying bodyguards. She was being held against her will and had no choice but to sleep with hundreds of men. She would never have even dreamed of becoming a prostitute if Jackie had not coerced her.

Besides the obvious emotional turmoil caused by her captivity at the house, Anuthida found herself being subjected to numerous virtual rapes by men who believed that just because they were paying for sex it gave them the right to abuse her in a brutal fashion.

On a number of occasions she was even forced to perform lesbian sex acts with the other girls at the house. Jackie warned her that if she didn't cooperate then she would authorize her friends back in Thailand to attack Anuthida's family. Mistress Jackie also insisted on taking pornographic photos of Anuthida and the other girls with their customers, which she later threatened to send to her family if she stepped out of line.

At night, as she bedded down on one of the single beds that she shared with another girl, Anuthida found that it had become particularly hard to sleep next to someone who she considered a friend yet had been obliged to have sexual contact with only a few hours previously.

Some days, Anuthida would look out of the windows of the house longingly at the children playing happily in the street, blissfully unware of the tortuous regime that existed inside that neat-looking home. She began to wonder whether she would ever experience normal life again. She even feared that Jackie would force her to stay on at the house even after her debt had been paid because she had proved so popular with the customers.

On Thursday, September 22, 1994, Sgt. Tom Budds of the Asian Organized Crime Unit of the LAPD, got word that the FBI had uncovered a vast Thai sex slave racket that spread across the United States. The house on Walnut Grove was run as a brothel, insisted three informants helping authorities in California.

Within a week, Budds and his colleagues had gathered enough information to feel confident of a prosecution if they were to arrest Jackie and the others at the house.

So, on Friday, September 30, Tom Budds obtained a search warrant from Whittier Municipal Court, signed by Judge Larry S. Knupp, and headed for Rosemead accompanied by six other investigators, including personnel from the U.S. customs department and the FBI.

In a carefully planned operation, Budds and his team sent in Thai-speaking agent Steve Tchen posing as a customer. After knocking on the front door, Jackie appeared and was about to show Tchen in when Budds and his colleague Deputy Hugh Lloyd appeared in their official sheriff's department raid jackets to announce they had a search warrant.

Jackie tried to slam the door shut, but Budds got his foot in the door before she could do so and the team entered the premises at high speed. Within seconds they found a customer in the front room, two Thai slave girls in a downstairs bedroom, two more upstairs, another one in bed with a naked customer, and another girl in the bathroom.

The girls were soon telling investigators that all-too-familiar horror story of how they had been trapped into becoming sex slaves for evil mistress Jackie and her boyfriend Tai Thahn Pham.

Over the following four hours, as Budds and his team conducted interviews with all the subjects in the garage area of the house, more than 30 customers continued to roll up to the property. Each was detained and interviewed and admitted that the going rate for sex with one of the slaves was $100. It also emerged that the services provided by Jackie had been promoted mainly through word of mouth in the tightly knit Asian community of L.A. and the surrounding cities.

Then, much to his horror, Sgt. Tom Budds discovered that Jackie and her bodyguards kept a large Taser gun in the front living room area of the house. It had been used to intimidate troublesome girls.

The house itself was sparsely furnished with just one couch in the living room area and a thin mattress on the floor of each of the bedrooms, plus a few closets with the girls' clothes in them.

Numerous other pieces of evidence were recovered

from the house by the investigators. Jackie Wood rapidly confessed to her role in the sex slave racket.

But another disturbing situation emerged when it was revealed that two other slave girls had escaped from the house in Rosemead just two days before the raid and they were being pursued by an angry "hit team" from Thailand who were determined to get revenge on the girls for daring to run away. They have never been located and it is genuinely feared that they may have been killed.

On October 3, felony charges were filed against Jackie Wood and her lover Pham. These included four counts each of pimping and pandering with a possible prison sentence of 32 years.

Wood was also charged with peonage (slavery) violation which could bring a two- to 10-year prison sentence.

Meanwhile, the slave girls found inside that house in Rosemead were held in protective custody to prevent any of Wood's associates from intimidating them before the trial of the suspects.

Additional charges of several counts of rape were made against Jackie Wood and Pham for having forced the girls to engage in sex. They faced life imprisonment if found guilty of those charges.

In January, 1995, both Wood and Pham pleaded guilty to pimping, pandering, and false imprisonment. Pham was sentenced to three years in prison while Wood got four years.

The pair pleaded guilty rather than face a trial and sentences of up to 30 years in prison if found guilty on all counts. As part of the deal, Pham and Wood also gave authorities information that may help track an organized crime operation believed to stretch from Asia to the western United States.

Authorities, who characterized the case as "slave trade 1990s-style," also revealed that the women imprisoned in the house were to be transported back to Thailand by the U.S. Immigration and Naturalization Service.

14

THE MARRIAGE "CONTRACT"

All spirits are enslaved, which serve things evil.
Shelley (1818)

Glynis Edmunds was feeling bored and restless in a tiny mining community. At 24 years of age, she felt she had the potential to get a good job, but the opportunities were few and far between in a place like West Lothian.

So when one of her girlfriends called up and said she was travelling down to London and would Glynis like to accompany her, she leapt at the opportunity, especially when her friend Denise said something about earning some money.

On the train south, Denise revealed to Glynis an extraordinary story about how she was actually travelling to London to take part in an arranged marriage for which she was going to get the not inconsiderable sum of 1,000 pounds ($1,500).

161

"I could probably get you a hubby," laughed Denise.

"For that kind of money I'd marry Frankenstein," said Glynis, a trim brunette.

Within a day of arriving in London, Glynis had been promised 800 pounds ($1,200) if she would marry a Polish waiter, enabling him to legally continue to live in Britain.

"It seemed like easy money and I couldn't see any harm in it at the time," explains Glynis.

In London, she and Denise stayed with a woman called Pam Sullivan at her house in the center of the city.

"For a couple of days we had a great time travelling around London and seeing the sights."

Denise "married" another Pole, a student called Stanley Pakula, at Westminster Register Office with Pam Sullivan acting as witness. Glynis was due to do likewise a few days later.

Then one evening, Pam introduced Denise and Glynis to a sharp-suited character who proudly and openly boasted that he was a pimp.

"He came over to Pam's place and brought a whole load of drugs, and we got completely loaded," explains Glynis. "I could hardly stand up by the end of the evening."

The young Scottish girl then made the mistake of sleeping with the pimp—and that was when her problems began.

In the middle of the night she stirred from her drug-induced slumber to find her hands bound together with a tie.

"I was terrified and started shouting and screaming for Pam, but the house was empty," recalls Glynis.

After struggling to get off the bed she discovered to her horror that the doors were double locked and she was trapped inside the house.

Glynis was distraught. She fell back onto the bed with her wrists still manacled and cried herself back to sleep.

At noon the next day, the pimp reappeared at the house and Glynis pleaded with him to release her.

"I started crying with desperation. Then he punched me in the face and called me a Scotch cow."

Glynis fell over on the floor after being hit and lay there with her wrists still tied.

The man grabbed her by the waist and forced her over on her stomach.

"Bitch. Fucking bitch," he muttered under his breath as he ripped down her panties and then unzipped his fly.

After satisfying his lust, the pimp told Glynis how sorry he was for being aggressive.

"If you're so sorry, why am I still tied up?" screamed Glynis, still in pain following his intimate earlier attack.

The pimp bent over her and untied her wrists.

"I said I was sorry and I meant it," said the man as he struggled to undo the tight knot.

Glynis felt a sense of overwhelming relief at her

"release." She tried to remain calm although her feisty Scottish character made her want to be very aggressive towards the pimp.

For the next few minutes they glanced at each other uncomfortably as Glynis tried to gather up her things so that she could move permanently out of that house.

Then the pimp glanced towards her and she could have sworn he had another smirk on his face.

"You fucking hate me, don't you?" he said.

"D'you blame me?" replied Glynis, whose pride was such that she couldn't resist telling him a few home truths. She regretted her comment the moment she looked at the expression on his face. It was almost identical to the way he had looked before he raped her earlier.

The pimp grabbed her. She struggled but could sense that the more she fought back the more he would hurt her.

This time he tied her ankles tightly together and pushed her face down on the smelly mattress in the corner of the room. At first, Glynis tried to kick out to stop him but each time she kicked him he retaliated with a crunching fist in her stomach. Then he dragged her off the mattress by her hair and started to smash her head on the wooden floor. She realized then that to resist was madness.

The next moment, he was forcing her mouth open with his fingers. She dreaded what he was about to do to her. She feared the worse. He poked one finger so far down her throat she almost vomited. Then she felt some kind of tablet being put in her mouth.

"Swallow it, you bitch. *Now!*" he screamed at her.

Glynis had no choice. She wanted to spit it out but knew that he would beat her senseless if she did not obey his command.

She rapidly lost her sense of balance and then became only vaguely aware of him starting to have sex with her once again.

Not long afterwards, Glynis Edmunds passed out.

She woke up the next morning covered with deep, dark bruises and congealed blood hanging off her nose from where he had attacked her.

"Get up," barked the pimp within seconds of Glynis opening her eyes. "I've got work for you."

He threw her clothes onto the mattress next to her.

"Hurry up. I've got a cabbie waiting outside."

"Fuck off," Glynis screamed back at the pimp.

"Shut up, bitch. You're mine until you wed that Polish guy next week. I own you. Try and run away and I'll come after you."

For the first time it dawned on Glynis that she was completely trapped. He was her slavemaster, and she knew that he meant every word he was saying.

Less than half an hour later, Glynis was bundled out of a taxi by the pimp into a rundown house.

At the top of three flights of creaking stairs they came to a door.

"Open up, Bob, it's me. I've got you a prezzie," shouted the pimp.

The door swung open and Bob stood there, well over 50 years old, a vast beer gut spilling over the top of his trousers and matted hair greasily combed forward to hide the onset of a balding pate.

His eyes snapped up and down Glynis's body and then he licked his sweaty lips.

"I owe you one, mate," said Bob as he grabbed Glynis by the hand and pulled her inside, leaving the pimp outside.

"Come with me," he said, his hand clammily holding her by the wrist as he led her to the far corner of the room where a filthy-looking double bed stood.

"Get your clothes off, love," said Bob. "I've got a few little surprises for you."

He pulled open the top drawer of a cheap-looking chest and pulled something out. Glynis didn't look up but she had a horrible feeling she knew what he was doing.

Bob threw a dildo on the bed, and it landed with a thump right next to Glynis.

"Pick it up and use it on yourself," he told her quietly but very firmly. "I can do what the fuck I want with you for the next hour or two."

After more than an hour of vile sex the man called Bob started complaining to his sex slave girl Glynis that she wasn't satisfying him properly.

Glynis, still high from the tablet that the pimp had forced down her earlier, could barely focus on the animal she had been made to sleep with.

Suddenly out of nowhere she felt Bob's fist crunch into her face, opening up the wound earlier inflicted by the pimp.

Glynis virtually lost consciousness when his fist connected, her balance went, and she fell off the bed, hitting her head on the floor as she keeled over.

When she came around a few hours later, Bob had gone but her pimp was back.

He told Glynis that he had plenty more where Bob came from.

"And if you give me any agro, I'll fucking kill you."

"But why are you doing this?"

"You're gonna make me some cash if it's the last thing I do."

The pimp then informed Glynis that her bogus marriage had been delayed for two weeks and so she would be his sex slave until the wedding.

Over the following 14 days, Glynis was forced to sleep with more than a dozen men.

"I was his sex slave. I had no choice. I could not escape because I genuinely feared he would hunt me down and kill me," recalls Glynis.

Many of the pimp's customers insisted on performing unnatural sex acts on Glynis, and at least five of them demanded bondage sessions during which she was tied up and whipped or beaten.

On the night before her bogus marriage finally took place, Glynis could not sleep because of the pain inflicted on her by the animals she had been forced to sleep with by the pimp.

Somehow, the pimp kept his word and released Glynis in time for her to go through her faked marriage to a Pole at Haringay Register Office, in North London.

She fled back to Scotland within hours of the ceremony, fearful that the pimp might change his mind and come after her.

15

A MADAM FOR ALL SEASONS

Slaves cannot breathe in England, if their lungs
Receive our air, that moment they are free;
They touch our country and their shackles fall.
The Task, William Cowper (1743-1809)

Camille Simmons-Ruiz looks more like a well-heeled businesswoman than a slave girl trader—but then that's because she is making a fortune out of forcing innocent young women to sell their bodies.

With her wire-framed spectacles, penchant for expensive power suits with rigid padded shoulders and $1,000 wristwatch, she commands her girls with nonstop discipline.

Simmons-Ruiz, who likes to be known as ''Randi'' to her clients, is proud of her ''business'' and the human cargo she deals in. Her apartment in one of London's most exclusive areas always has at least three pretty young slave girls ready and waiting for any of her hundreds of male and female customers.

Randi prefers to offer teenage girls for sex because many of her clients like them to pretend they are schoolgirls. The younger women are also much easier for Randi to intimidate if they try to escape.

These innocent girls are smuggled into Britain from southeast Asia, imprisoned in her apartment, and forced to commit appalling sex acts with wealthy customers who often pay Randi as much as 1,000 pounds for a single session.

The girls enter the country on visas bought for $1,500 each from crooked senior employees of the British embassies in places like Bangkok and Rangoon. Once in London, they are forbidden to leave the apartment or even to use the telephone.

Randi splashes out 10,000-pound fees to her agents in places like Thailand, which includes door-to-door delivery of the girls to her apartment from halfway across the globe.

The girls are provided to Randi on bizarre six-month contracts that she devised because ''most of them run out of steam after that period of time so it is better to get replacements.''

Randi even openly admits she is a ruthless taskmaster—but then she should know because she was a slave girl herself once.

''Because of my investment I have to keep them under proper control and make sure they work efficiently,'' she says. ''By not staying any longer than six months they don't even have time to make friends, which is perfect. I don't want them running off before the contract has finished. They're here to make me money.''

Randi is netting thousands of pounds a week from her slave girl racket, which services at least 10 men every day at the well-appointed apartment she rents near Marble Arch, just a stone's throw from the Queen of England's home at Buckingham Palace.

Randi's sordid business attracts many customers by advertising on cards distributed in telephone kiosks in London's West End. She even promotes the girls as being ''beautiful new Japanese students.''

In the one-year period up to October 1995, Randi took delivery of 17 slave girls from the dirt-poor provinces of some of the poorest countries in southeast Asia.

They are lured over to London with the promise of reasonably paid secretarial jobs only to arrive and have their passports confiscated by their new boss Randi, who even employs English women as ''maids'' to keep an eye on them and make sure they do as she commands.

Randi also ''sublets'' some of the more trusted girls out to other escort agencies and massage parlors in London, knowing full well that they will not try to escape because she has retained their travel documents.

''Each girl costs me about 10,000 pounds, and my people in Thailand make all the arrangements and will deliver them to any address you'd like in Britain.

When they arrive I get a phone call and collect them from whatever hotel they're waiting in. An escort brings them over to make sure they get through immigration without any hassles.

"There haven't been any problems so far because the visas are genuine. They have got someone inside the embassies to fix that for them."

Randi, 42, personally trains the girls on arrival in Britain. As a former sex slave girl herself she says she knows all the tricks.

"They have to give a man pleasure, otherwise he will not want to come back, and repeat business is the key to this trade."

Randi, who is bisexual, even "breaks in" some of her favorite girls and insists, "Sure, I own them and I guess they are slaves, but I tell them to just get on with it because they won't be with me for that long."

Until only two years ago, Randi herself worked at a sex sauna in Stratford, East London.

If they are lucky, the girls who work for Randi receive a small payoff at the end of their six-month stint in London. But the fact remains that they are effectively slaves because they are not free to leave her sordid business.

As one girl says, "We come to England expecting a proper job and then get told we have no choice but to work as prostitutes. It is degrading and depressing, and we are definitely slaves. There is no other word for it."

*   *   *

The evil slave girl network that supplies women for mistresses like Randi is worth revealing in more detail because these so-called "agents" are reckoned to be supplying sex slaves to the United States, Japan, Malaysia, and Singapore, as well as numerous other European countries besides Britain.

The racket is backed by organizations like the Thai mafia, and the girls know that any attempt to escape will provoke violent retaliation on their families back home.

One of the "slave lords" in Thailand is a 42-year-old known as the "Fat Man" to clients like mistress Randi. He owns a business exporting bamboo chopsticks and toothpicks.

The Fat Man and his wife run their lucrative vice sideline from their home near Bangkok Airport. He frequently travels to capital cities like London, Washington, and Tokyo to escort recruits to their new vice bosses.

Every visit has been immensely succcessful. At London's Heathrow Airport, for example, the girls are always waved straight through after the immigration officer stamps the date of entry on their passports. "I go with them to answer any awkward questions," he says.

The Fat Man claims that getting visas at the British Embassy in Bangkok is "Very easy. It's actually easier than finding good quality girls! We pay 40,000 baht [$1,500] for each visa.

"The girls have no money, so we fake job references and details of bank accounts, so everything looks official. We don't need any money up front. The clients pay cash on delivery when the girls arrive in England with their suitcases.''

The Fat Man insists that he has ''girls on tap'' whom he can coerce into going abroad at a few days' notice.

''They think it's the beginning of a dream existence in a new country. They never question us closely about the type of job that might be available. They are that desperate.''

The slave girls themselves often turn out to be naive women who have never been further afield than their own village.

But the Fat Man is always on the lookout for some very special girls: virgins. He claims they are worth at least a third more to clients like mistress Randi. And he even boasts that one attractive 16-year-old virgin was sold on from one mistress to another three times at a profit until she was sold directly to an Arab client who flew her to his home in the Middle East and kept her prisoner there for seven months.

The Fat Man's team in Thailand consists of a bizarre group of criminals whose duties read like something out of a novel.

Ed procures gullible girls from the provinces. Veron hides them in safe houses while their travel documents are being prepared. Then there is a man called Moo, a master forger whose skills provide much of the false documentation.

*   *   *

Back in London, one of the girls forced into prostitution by evil mistress Randi reveals how her brutal regime kept her trapped in that sordid den of sexual depravity.

"I was tricked into travelling to London and then forced by Randi to be a hooker. Randi promised that it would all turn out okay because I would earn enough money to go home and buy my parents a house," explained slave girl Lao.

"But Randi took all the money directly off the clients and never gave any of it to me. When I threatened to go, she raped me with a sex aid and then tied me to a chair for two days."

Lao, 19, says that she then realized she could not escape from Randi's clutches "because she knew where my family were and threatened to have them killed if I tried to make a run for it."

Lao, from one of the poorest regions of South Vietnam, discloses some of the appalling sex acts she was forced to perform for some of Randi's perverted clients.

"One time, Randi got me to go to this Japanese businessman's house in Belgravia with another of her girls called Ty," explains Lao. "When we got there, we found that he had invited seven male friends round to the house, and he expected us to sleep with all of them. When I refused he and two of the other men got very nasty and beat me while two of the others raped the other girl.

"Then they raped me and beat her. It was horrible. Then when they finished, instead of letting us go they locked us in a room together and insisted we sleep with each other while they took it in turns to watch us through the keyhole.

"At first, we halfheartedly kissed and cuddled on the bed. Then the host burst into the room and started beating us both with a horsewhip because he said we were not doing it properly.

"Then we had to promise to have full sex with each other. It was disgusting. We could hear them breathing and moaning outside the door as they watched. They even left the phone off the hook so some of them could listen from an extension.

"Every now and again one of them would shout obscenities at us through the door. They even made us talk dirty to each other so they could hear."

But Lao and Ty's ordeal did not finish there.

Lao continues, "After more than an hour trapped in that room, all eight of the men came in and raped us in turn. We held hands throughout and shut our eyes and tried not to think about what was happening. But I will never forget it as long as I live."

Lao finally escaped from Randi's evil clutches by pretending her mother back in Vietnam was dying from cancer. The debauched mistress uncharacteristically took pity on the young girl and allowed her to leave.

"Randi used to always say she fancied me, and I am certain she had a soft spot for me. I think that's why she let me go."

Others have not been so lucky.

Ty finally left Randi after six months, penniless and

badly beaten after quarreling with her mistress. She was so desperate to survive that she had to go and work as a street hooker and has never had a normal job since.

"Not only does Randi turn us into sex slaves but she effectively ruins most of our lives forever. She is the sickest woman I have ever met," adds Lao.

16

BEHIND CLOSED DOORS

There is no doubt that slavery is taking place in England. Who would have thought that such a state of affairs is possible?
Lord Longford, speaking in Britain's House of Lords on November 28, 1990

———

BEXLEYHEATH, KENT, ENGLAND, FALL, 1990

Leafy suburban streets dominate this town on the edge of south London. Homes tend to be semi-detached. Gardens are always immaculately groomed with neatly clipped hedges and well-mowed lawns. There is also a prolific number of net curtains in front windows—perfect for nosey neighbours to keep an eye on their fellow residents.

Bexleyheath is certainly not the type of place one would expect to find a slave girl, but then you should never judge a book by its cover.

Dr. Truman Abassah, a respected surgeon at a local hospital, and his health-worker wife seemed on the

179

surface to be the sort of residents that towns like Bexleyheath thrive on: middle class, reserved, and very,
very polite. There were never any parties or loud music at the Abassahs' spacious four-bedroom house.

But behind the closed doors of that comfortable
house all kinds of terrors were being inflicted in the
name of domestic servitude. For Dr. Abassah and his
wife Philomena had a propensity for sadistic violence
when it came to dealing with their maid Helen Samuels.

And on one particular afternoon, Mrs. Abassah had
a very twisted motive for attacking her servant: She
believed the girl was having an affair with her husband.

"I know you've been to bed with him. I know,"
muttered Philomena to the terrified 25-year-old Helen.
The young woman had endured almost four years of
torture, beatings, starvation, and neglect at the hands
of her master and mistress, but this latest development
had shocked her.

A few minutes earlier, Philomena had arrived home
unexpectedly early from work to find Helen sitting in
the kitchen. That alone had sparked a mini-explosion
because Helen was usually locked outside when the
couple went off to work in the morning. They had
told their slave girl that they didn't trust her in the
house on her own.

Helen had discovered a spare key some months
previously and would slip into the house after her
mistress had departed, always making sure she was

back outside in the yard by the time Philomena returned.

"Never. Never come inside this house again when I am not here. Do you understand, girl?" Philomena bellowed at the poor creature.

That was when she had thrown in the extraordinary accusation about Helen having an affair with Dr. Abassah. It was ludicrous from Helen's point of view because she loathed him as much as she hated Philomena. But the problem was that she had been enduring regular sexual harassment from the doctor since the first week she had arrived at the household.

It started with wandering hands and had progressed to the point where Dr. Abassah would deliberately ensure he could catch Helen alone at least once a week for some sick self-gratification.

"If you lay another finger on him I'll kill you," screamed Philomena at her muted servant. "I know he's in love with you."

Philomena took a long breath then, almost as if she was trying to convince herself before she continued.

"I've seen the way he looks at you. I know the signs. It's not the first time, you know."

Philomena wasn't looking for a response from Helen. She had long since forbidden her maid from talking back to her unless asked a specific question. She just enjoyed hearing the sound of her own voice.

"I've never trusted you. I think you want him to yourself. Well, you're not going to get him—"

She stopped mid-sentence. The front door slamming shut signified a sudden end to her monologue. The doctor was home.

Dr. Abassah was a neat, bespectacled, round figure with a fondness for three-piece suits even on the hottest summer day. He had that typical doctor's habit of bringing his bedside manners home with him. In other words, he skimmed over the top of potential problems at home by always replying to his wife's outbursts with the sweetest, "Oh, you're absolutely right, my darling."

As he walked into the kitchen that day, he undoubtedly sensed the tension in the air, but then that was nothing new inside the Abassah household. Violence ruled with a rod of iron.

The doctor greeted his wife fondly and swiftly retreated to his upstairs office. This was one argument he had the good sense to keep out of.

Philomena continued fuming. "I've seen the way he looks at you. Pure lust, and you are encouraging him. Touch him again and you're dead."

Poor Helen stood there shaking. She was too scared to respond. She knew that her mistress was spoiling for a fight and it would be a battle that only Philomena could win.

But Helen's silence further fueled the fire as far as Philomena was concerned. Her teeth were grating at a furious rate. She stared maniacally at her servant.

"Get out! Don't come back until the morning," she screamed.

Helen moved off towards the back door to the garden and the slab of pavement that had become her cold and miserable night-time retreat.

Suddenly, Philomena lunged at her slave girl, forcing her to the ground. Then she straddled the girl, who was lying facedown, and began to squeeze her round the neck. Her nails were digging deep into Helen's flesh and the pain was excruciating. Then Helen started to lose her breath.

"Bitch. I know. I know . . ."

At that moment, Dr. Abassah appeared in the kitchen looking completely unconcerned that his wife was on the floor throttling the maid. He said nothing and just moved quietly across the room to a cabinet where he took out a glass and poured himself some milk.

He glanced down at the vicious assault being committed not two feet away and smiled a brief, greasy smile.

"Darling, do we have any biscuits anywhere?"

Philomena stopped her strangling exercise in midflight.

"Try the pantry."

Dr. Abassah shuffled off, and Philomena decided to halt her latest attempt to hurt Helen.

She stood up, brushed down her dress, and did not utter a word to her maid.

Helen rushed for the back door. The near-freezing temperatures outside were far preferable to anything that was happening inside that terrible house.

* * *

It hadn't always been so awful at the Abassahs'. When Helen first started with them in 1985, the couple simply ignored their maid, even though she was actually a distant relative.

Helen had first encountered her new master and mistress when she was living in her home country of Nigeria. Her aunt was Mrs. Abassah's stepmother, and when Philomena suggested she might like to join her and her husband in England, Helen leapt at the chance.

But within weeks of arriving in Britain strange things started to happen. To begin with, Helen, whose mother had died many years previously, only received one letter from her family back home. It came from her brother warning her never to return to Nigeria because her aunt had been so upset at her decision to leave and work for the Abassahs that she had disowned her.

Unfortunately, Helen's master and mistress were not in the slightest bit interested in her family problems back home. They barked at her and insisted she work morning, noon, and night. But at least she had a roof over her head and a means to survive.

But then one day Philomena started shouting at Helen about the dirty kitchen floor. She got angrier and angrier. That was when she hit Helen for the first time.

A couple of days later, she gave her a severe thrashing with a stick because she didn't like the way Helen had stacked the clean dishes.

Helen thought about running away, but she had no

friends and nowhere to go. One time she even got as far as the nearest railway station only to turn round when she realized she did not even have enough cash to pay for a ticket into London.

When she got home, the doctor and his wife were waiting for her.

"How dare you leave this house without my permission," said Abassah in a cold, steely tone. His wife looked on with a self-satisfying grin on her face. She knew what was coming next.

"Come here, girl," beckoned the doctor. His breathing had changed pace. "Bend over the table. I'm going to teach you some manners."

Helen closed her eyes and tried to think about something else. She felt his hand grab her flesh and squeeze. What was happening?

Just then the doctor crashed the palm of his hand across her backside. Then he grabbed a book from the table next to her and started smashing it on the backs of her thighs.

Helen opened her eyes slightly and looked across the room at Philomena. She was smirking, clearly enjoying every moment of her husband's abusive actions.

Within a few months of that first attack, Helen became so used to the beatings inflicted on her by the doctor and his wife that she would be relieved if he only used his fists rather than an actual weapon.

Then one day, the doctor exploded in rage against Helen because she could not find his slippers.

After the customary spanking on her backside,

Abassah insisted his slave should lie on the floor of the living room on her back. A shiver of trepidation shook through Helen's entire body. She feared the worst.

"Don't move, girl," barked the doctor.

Then he opened the drawer of a nearby bureau and took something out. It was a large safety pin.

Helen started shaking even more profusely.

"Don't move," repeated the doctor as if he was about to inject a patient with medicine.

Just then, Helen felt a sharp stabbing sensation in her side. Then another in her shoulder. Then another in her breast. He was stabbing her with the safety pin at a furious rate. Short, sharp pains were breeding all over her body as he quickened to a sickening pace.

Ten minutes later he stopped after at least one hundred little wounds had been inflicted, leaving speckles of blood on her T-shirt and jeans. Helen was terrified and ran from the room.

During another beating, Helen was hit on the head with a tray by Philomena until fragments of it were buried in her scalp.

"You're bleeding on the carpet. Get out!" screamed Philomena hysterically following the crazed attack.

Helen recalls, "I went to the bathroom to bathe my head and put my face right into the water. It was dark red with my blood."

Dr. Abassah, who worked at South London's Brook Hospital, and his wife, a personnel officer with

Greenwich Health Authority, then began a new regime of starving Helen into submission.

Before going to work they would check all the food in their house.

"If I touched the food I would get a beating when they came home," says Helen. "I began to eat apples and pears from the garden although they were often unripe."

And when the Abassahs did give their slave girl anything to eat it would invariably have already gone beyond its expiration date.

"I remember Philomena telling me to drink milk that was sour. It was watery and there were lumps in it."

As a further punishment, Helen was regularly forced to wash her mouth out with water containing sterilizing tablets.

By this time Helen weighed less than 90 pounds, and hardly an inch of her body was unmarked from the beatings.

She was also forced to sleep outside the back door, mainly because Philomena was becoming so paranoid about her husband having an affair with the slave girl.

One day Helen became so hungry she left a begging note for the next-door neighbors, Doris and Reg Tapley. It read, "PLEASE HELP ME BY LEAVING BREAD OR BISCUITS BY YOUR DOOR."

It was Helen's first message to the outside world. The Tapleys were understandably shocked by the situation. They had heard a few crying sounds coming from the house but never frequently enough to warrant any investigation.

However, they had noticed that Helen was sleeping outside, even in winter, and it was clear something strange was happening inside the house.

Eventually, the Tapleys alerted the police and the Abassahs were arrested.

Dr. Abassah and his wife Philomena were eventually jailed for five years for torturing and starving Helen Samuels. They were also ordered to be deported back to Nigeria after they had completed their sentences.

Judge Jonathan Van Der Werff said it was difficult to understand how a doctor could have inflicted such suffering on a young girl.

The court heard that Helen had worked at least 13 hours a day, seven days a week, and never received a penny in wages.

Her rescuers, Doris and Reg Tapley, became Helen's close friends after her release from captivity. Mrs. Tapley said, "I really hope they give her a fair chance, especially if they consider what she's been through.

"Anyone who saw her when she was taken away by the police would have felt as sick as I did. I feel Helen is very lucky to be alive."

Helen herself says that life with the Abassahs "made me wish I was dead." She adds, "I cannot forgive them."

Detective Constable Stephen Westwood says the case was "shocking," adding, "I've never seen anything like this before. I was horrified and couldn't believe this could happen in this country.''

Helen has now recovered sufficiently from her ordeal to start a new life in south London where she has been attending night classes in dressmaking.

She says simply, ''I did whatever the Abassahs said because I was frightened for my life. I used to lie at night and pray, saying to God, if this is the way You want it, I'll put up with it. But if it isn't then please, please make it stop.''

17

VICE TRAP

Crime and punishment grow out of one stem.
Emerson (1841)

For more than ten years, British girls have been lured into a life of vice in this immensely popular resort area. Naive youngsters all too often fly out to the sunshine coast on vacation looking for fun, adventure, and romance.

Many even hope to settle down to a glamorous lifestyle with the chance of a glittering career a million miles away from the welfare lines and freezing temperatures back in Britain.

But for one such girl, those dreams fell cruelly apart when she became trapped in a den of depravity from which there was no escape. This is her story.

Paula O'Neill's decision to turn her life around and move to the Costa Del Sol was greeted with great indifference by her family in the British town of Luton, Bedfordshire, just north of London.

"Why don't you get a proper job?" asked her father, just minutes after Paula, 22, announced she had been hired by a time-share company to sell apartments on a complex near Marbella.

"That's boring, Dad. I want some adventure," replied Paula. She meant every word.

However, within two weeks of arriving in Spain, she started to regret that bold statement.

For her job selling shares in apartments entailed a hell of a lot more persuasion of clients than Paula had ever imagined. Some of the other girls she met on the complex the first day of her new job even suggested that the only way to make a quick sale and earn some hefty commissions was to sleep with prospective male clients.

Paula was appalled at the prospect and after fruitlessly trying to prove her point by getting a "straight" sale without any sexual enticement, she quit in disgust.

The problem was that the job had come with a free apartment and that meant she was out on the streets with only a few hundred pounds in savings and a handful of phone numbers of friends of friends.

Paula's pride prevented her from returning home. She had a point to prove to her folks and she was determined not to give up at the first hurdle.

She checked into a cheap hotel and started looking

for work. It wasn't as easy as she thought. She spoke no Spanish and there had been a recent backlash against the British in the area, which had resulted in a spirit of non-cooperation when it came to locals employing anyone with an English accent.

One night, down on her luck and feeling very sorry for herself, Paula arranged to meet a girlfriend from the time-share business for a drink at the picturesque port area on the edge of Marbella.

It was a steaming hot evening, and thousands of revellers were packing the narrow streets, pouring in and out of the numerous bars, clubs, and casinos. Paula's friend never showed up that night, but she enjoyed a few drinks, chatted with a charming Arab from one of the yachts in the harbor, and tried to forget all about her troubles.

By midnight, Paula and her new friend who called himself Ali had been joined by a couple of other English girls. Paula found them a little too forward for her liking. She reckoned they might have been high-class hookers, many of whom wandered in and out of the bars in the port looking for rich customers.

With the sangria flowing and everyone in high spirits, Paula did not object when Ali suggested all the girls might like to come aboard his yacht for a nightcap. What could possibly happen? she wondered. There were three of them against one man after all.

As the party stumbled up the gangplank to the vast

120-foot yacht with its whirling radar scanner, Paula remembers taking off her black stilettos because the heels kept getting stuck in the wooden ridges on the deck.

She cannot remember another thing after that until she woke up the next morning to find herself tied to a bed and stripped of her clothes. Something was covering her mouth as well.

"I thought I was dreaming. I shut my eyes tightly and then opened them slowly once again. But I was still there," she recalls.

"There was a rocking sensation and I realized I was still on the yacht, and it was out at sea."

Just then, two men walked into the room. Paula shut her eyes and listened. One of them was the man who called himself Ali, and the other was an older Arab in a headdress and flowing white robes. He looked at least 60 years of age.

Paula opened her eyes just enough to see them. She prayed they would think she was still unconscious because she needed time to think what to do.

They were speaking in Arabic and it was very heated. Suddenly the older man started prodding Ali in the shoulder angrily. Ali then stormed out of the room. The man walked towards her, smiling.

"You're awake," he said pointedly.

Paula did not stir in the hope he would go away. But she knew he knew she was pretending.

He sat on the edge of bed and ran a hand slowly up the inside of her thigh. Paula could feel the goose bumps appearing.

"Wake up. It's time," said the old Arab. His hand stopped at the top of her thigh. Then he pinched her flesh hard.

Paula's eyes snapped open angrily. He smiled.

She tried to move but the ropes around her wrists and ankles stung painfully as they tightened.

His hand moved to her face and he ran a finger across her lips. It tickled in a nasty kind of way. Paula started hyperventilating with a combination of fear and awkwardness. She couldn't talk because a black silk scarf was gagging her.

"You're beautiful," he muttered as his eyes panned up and down her body.

Paula then started really fidgeting. She wanted him to know she was not about to give up her body without a fight. But she also felt horribly vulnerable, lying there naked.

He undid the gag.

Paula spluttered for breath. "You bastard. Let me go." She spat the words out contemptuously. He seemed even happier at her outburst.

"You English girls are so spirited."

He bent down and tried to kiss her on the lips. She bit him hard. He reacted furiously and hit her across the face with the back of his hand.

"Now, it's time . . ."

Three hours later, the old Arab finally left the room. Paula's entire face was horribly bitten and bruised. She was crying. Then Ali entered.

"I am sorry if he was rough with you, but that is his way," he said.

"Let me go, you bastard," she screamed through her tears.

"I cannot do that yet. He wants you to stay for a few days."

"I'd rather die," Paula told Ali defiantly.

He then sat down on the end of the bed and admitted that her drinks had been deliberately drugged that night in the bar and she was basically their prisoner. "You'll survive this if you cooperate. We pay very generously."

"Fuck your money and fuck you. Just drop me at the nearest port," said Paula, but she knew that wouldn't happen.

She was being held captive, and they could do whatever they liked to her.

Later that day, the older Arab returned and carried on where he had left off earlier. Paula turned her head to one side and prayed that it would soon end.

Paula O'Neill's ordeal went on for three more agonizing days. At times she felt like fighting back, but she eventually became resigned to her fate, acknowledging that it was probably the key to her survival.

Eventually the old Arab grew bored of her, and she was dropped back at Marbella port. Ali gave her 5,000 pounds. She tried to throw it back at him at first.

But then he said, "Take it. It'll help you survive. It's tough out here."

"I'm not a hooker. I don't do it for money."

"That's not the point," said Ali. "If you want to avoid being taken prisoner again you should take the money."

Paula hated herself for it, but she kept the cash. She went back to her hotel, showered, cried, ate, and then cried again.

"I hated myself even more than I hated them. But I had to survive."

Within two months of her sex slave ordeal, Paula became a full-time call girl on the Costa Del Sol. After all that fighting, she had given up the battle.

"One night I bumped into those same girls who were with me when Ali drugged my drink. They introduced me to a madam called Candy in a bar. She said I could earn a fortune because English girls were in big demand, especially with Arabs."

Candy helped set Paula up in a rented apartment with three other girls in the center of Marbella.

"It's strange the way things have turned out. Those three or four days on the yacht were a living nightmare I shall never forget, yet my experiences numbed me about everything else.

"I just don't think about the same sort of things anymore. I have a life to live. It's not nice being a prostitute and I am certain I never would have become one if I hadn't have been taken prisoner by that Arab.

"But it seems to me that there are only two types of people in this world, the givers and the takers. I tried the honest way and it failed. Now I don't give a damn about anyone but myself."

18

WITH THIS RING...

He only may chastise who loves.
Rabindranath Tagore (1913)

———

It is a typical German town with buildings dating back to the fifteenth century and a sheer grayness that is daunting to any visitor. Numerous tidy apartment blocks, never more than ten stories in height, provide a severe backdrop while the townsfolk rarely smile and tend to get on with the job at hand.

Provincial German towns frequently have that cold atmosphere in the daytime and seem to only come alive when darkness has fallen and the nightlife takes over to become the lifeblood of virtually every male under the age of 60.

There is a commonly held theory about this stark contrast: the Germans work very hard to earn a living, which means they tend to play even harder.

A night on the town in Braunschweig was usually

a three-stage affair for the typical lively male resident out with his friends.

Naturally, food would come first and that usually meant a vast three- or four-course meal in one of the town's many restaurants. Sauerkraut and sausages, lashings of roast pork. All washed down with huge liter mugs of beer.

Then your typical group would wander off to one of the livelier bars in Braunschweig where they would regale each other with blustery tales of woe covering a range of topics from soccer to politics.

By about 9:30 everyone would be well and truly on the way to drink-induced euphoria. This was when the insatiable appetite for sex usually took over.

Men would flock to the brothels on the edge of Braunschweig. All the townsfolk knew they were there, but they didn't want to hear about or ever publicly acknowledge their existence.

Names like ''The Pink Pussycat'' and ''The L.A. Club'' were popular. The Germans have always felt more reassured by brothels with American-sounding names. They like those glamourous titles because that makes them feel they are the *real* thing.

But the setup in each of those houses of ill-repute was basically the same: the customers paid a nominal entrance fee. They then would stroll up to the bar and order a drink. Suddenly, at least six girls, in skimpy basques, stockings, and stilettos would appear as if by magic and start flirting outrageously.

Men on their first visit nearly always actually believed the girls were genuinely interested in their good looks and magnetic personalities. The fact that the girls were virtually naked and were more concerned with how much cash they could earn seemed irrelevant.

Deitmar Abke and Bernd Czerwinsky were two of the more experienced members of the brothel scene in Braunschweig in the fall of 1994. Both of them were well known in some of the more brutal, sadomasochistic brothels where customers demanded some appallingly perverted practices.

The fact that Deitmar, 31, had been married to a gorgeous blonde girl called Marita for more than a year did absolutely nothing to curtail his sexual demands as far as the dominatrixes of Braunschweig were concerned.

Meanwhile, bachelor Czerwinsky's sick and twisted sexual habits had become so excessive that many of the prostitutes he encountered refused to have sex with him.

Czerwinksy was particularly fond of beating girls with a bullwhip until they bled. He was also renowned for being an extremely penny-pinching guy who would always try to beat the girls down on money while expecting to beat them to a pulp in reality.

Czerwinsky's sexual depravity had gotten so unpleasant by the middle of 1994 that he was actually finding it virtually impossible to hire a prostitute to put up with his demands.

Meanwhile, his weaker, married friend Deitmar Abke was starting to get clumsy with the perpetual lies he told his wife about where he went until the early hours most Friday and Saturday nights.

Marita Abke was a real head-turner and she was starting to grow rather frustrated by her husband's complete refusal to include her in any of his social activities. Even worse, he would arrive home so drunk in the early hours of the morning that he was incapable of making love to her.

Inevitably, Marita started to get very irritated by her new husband. She began to interrogate him about his habits. This annoyed Abke a great deal because he felt it was none of her business.

"I pay the rent and I make sure you have a good life. What is your problem, woman?" he screamed at her drunkenly after arriving home from some brothel or other early one morning.

"I know you have another woman, Deitmar. It's so obvious. Why don't you admit it?" Marita yelled back furiously.

Within seconds, Deitmar was snoring his head off and poor Marita was left to fester furiously about the state of her marriage.

The fights between the couple not surprisingly grew more and more heated as the months progressed.

And on his regular trips to the brothels, Deitmar found himself growing increasingly violent towards the prostitutes he slept with. It was almost as if he was taking out his anger and frustration on them rather than his wife.

Meanwhile, his friend Bernd Czerwinsky was getting equally frustrated by the fact that he was having more and more difficulty finding a prostitute prepared to put up with the horrendous beatings he wanted to inflict on them.

One night the two men were drowning their sorrows before yet another sortie to a brothel when Deitmar surprised his friend by starting to openly criticize his wife.

"I'm fed up with her nagging. She just won't leave me alone. She thinks I've got a girlfriend. It's getting ridiculous," he explained to Czerwinsky.

In Deitmar's mind, sleeping with prostitutes did not count as adultery. He simply saw them as providing a service for a guy who knew he couldn't get his sexual kicks at home.

Czerwinsky was actually rather jealous of his friend because he seemed to have the best of both worlds. He had a beautiful wife at home and a number of prostitutes on tap. Czerwinsky was particularly envious because he had always thought that Marita was incredibly attractive.

"You don't know how lucky you are," said Czerwinsky. "If I had a wife like Marita—"

"You'd beat the shit out of her," laughed Deitmar. "I know what turns you on."

Czerwinsky hit back coolly. "You're dead right, I would."

A brief beat of silence between the two friends followed. Then Czerwinsky took a deep breath before continuing.

"If you're so pissed off with her, I'll take her off your hands."

"What?" exclaimed an astonished Abke.

"I mean it. I think she's an incredibly sexy girl. I've always fancied her."

"No way."

"It's just a thought. Nothing more."

Abke quickly changed the subject, but he knew full well that his friend meant every word.

A few beers later, the conversation returned to Marita.

"Did you mean it?" asked Deitmar.

"Mean what?"

"That you'd take Marita off my hands."

"Of course I did. I'd pay you a lot of money to have my way with her."

"You're kidding."

"You want to bet?"

"How much?"

"Fifty thousand."

Deitmar Abke paused for a second as he absorbed the significance of their conversation. His best friend had just offered him 50,000 marks to have sex with his wife. It seemed like the perfect answer. He would be rid of her nagging ways and he'd make some much-needed extra cash.

Just then Czerwinsky butted in. "But you'd have to let me do what I want to her. I might keep her for days. You can have her back whenever I don't need her."

Abke knew perfectly well what his friend would do to his wife, yet he found the scheme very appealing except for one big problem.

"She'd never agree."

"She would if you had some hold over her. Like threatening to kill her parents if she didn't co-operate."

By the end of that evening this dreadful, perverted deal had been struck and Marita Abke's fate was sealed.

The following night Abke explained to his wife what he had done. Not surprisingly, she went wild with anger. That's a pity, thought Abke, it means I'll have to tie her up. He then bundled her into the back of his car and drove her to Czerwinsky's apartment on the other side of town.

Once inside the flat, he pushed his terrified wife on the bed and then demanded his 50,000 marks. Czerwinsky paid up immediately and told his friend to leave.

"I'll call you when I've finished with her," he said, looking hungrily down at Marita.

Abke did not feel a twinge of guilt and left the apartment immediately. That will teach her a lesson she'll never forget, he thought to himself.

Less than an hour later, Marita Abke was being locked in wooden stocks in a torture room that Czerwinsky had created to try and feed his evil habits.

When she screamed, he shoved a leather hood over her head and then laughed before he submitted her to the first of many painful beatings.

For the following two days, Marita was abused in such a vicious fashion that it would be insensitive to repeat any of the details here. But suffice to say, Czerwinsky's perverted habits knew no boundaries. At one stage he even hired a prostitute to beat Marita while he watched. He also forced her to drink alcohol and take drugs.

By the time she was returned to her husband, Marita was a quivering wreck. It took her more than a week to recover from her ordeal and return to her job as a secretary. She thought about telling her colleagues what had happened but kept thinking back to her husband's threat to kill her parents if she dared tell anyone.

Back at home, she shook with fear each time the telephone rang in case it was Czerwinsky calling up. Strangely, her husband Deitmar had actually been nicer to her since he had struck up the dreadful deal with his friend. Marita suspected it was because he was rather turned on by the thought of his wife getting beaten black and blue by another man.

A few days later, Czerwinsky called up and demanded that Marita be made available for another debauched sex session. This time, Marita pleaded with her husband not to make her go.

"I can't stand it. It's so horrible. Please, I'll do anything if you tell him I can't do it. Please."

But Abke would not budge. "I made a deal with Bernd and I don't see why I should go back on it."

Marita then flung herself at her husband's feet.

"You can't do this to me. You can't."

"I can," said Abke as he felt inside his pocket for something.

"Now you'd better do as I say."

But Marita was shaking her head furiously.

"No. No. No."

Abke flicked on his cigarette lighter and held it under his wife's wrist. She screamed, but he held her wrist firmly in one hand while burning it with the other.

"Yes, you will."

These dreadful sex sessions with the sick and twisted sadist Czerwinsky went on for months and eventually Marita went into a zombielike state every time her husband forced her to go to his friend's torture chamber apartment.

Her wrists were scarred from where she had been forced to sit in the wooden stocks and her body was covered in bruises and cuts from the beatings he had inflicted on her.

In a strange way, she had been beaten into submission. She no longer fought against her husband, but he still insisted on trussing her up like a turkey before taking her round to Czerwinsky's cold and damp apartment.

At home, there was virtually no communication between Marita and her husband. He had started prowling the red-light districts of the town virtually every night and she would be so exhausted from the stress and fear which ruled her life that she would usually fall asleep by 10 each evening.

* * *

This time it was Deitmar Abke who had the look of sheer terror on his face. Marita smiled with satisfaction. A few minutes earlier, she had smashed him over the head with a hammer as he walked into their home. Now he was the one trussed up with rope to a chair that stood in the middle of the living room.

She walked around and around her husband and smacked him on the face every few seconds.

''I haven't decided what I'm going to do with you, but it will hurt more than anything I have had to put with,'' Marita screamed at her husband.

Abke looked pale and pathetic. Marita picked up a rolling pin and smashed it against the side of his face. She could hear the teeth cracking. Her husband sobbed and pleaded for mercy.

''Bastard. You're going to pay for what you've done to me,'' muttered Marita.

Just then she awoke from her dream. To anyone else it would have been a nightmare, but to Marita it was to provide inspiration. She had enjoyed that dream so much that she knew she had to get a grip of herself and do something to stop her husband and his evil friend from continuing to use her as a sex slave.

She lay in bed and started to formulate a plan. Each time she thought about how to punish her husband it got worse. By the time she had finalized her scheme, he was going to pay the ultimate price.

* * *

The following evening, Marita was waiting for her husband to come home from work so she could go through with her revenge. When he finally appeared she attacked him so swiftly with a carving knife that he was dead from a dozen stab wounds before he even knew what had happened.

Then Marita decided to disembowel her husband and rid herself of every piece of him forever. She started cutting his flesh into tiny pieces but found herself overwhelmed with guilt about what she had just done.

A few days later, she confessed to police that she had murdered her husband. But when detectives heard about her horrific life at the hands of Abke and Czerwinsky they promised her they would do everything in their power to help her.

In October, 1995, at a court in Braunschweig, Marita admitted killing her husband but the judge set her free after hearing about her hellish life at the hands of these two sadistic monsters.

19

SOLD BY HER FAMILY

Take this sorrow to thy heart, and make it a part of thee, and it shall nourish thee till thou art strong again.
    Longfellow, *Hyperion* (1839)

———

It's a sprawling city skirted by some of the worst shantytowns in the world. Yet ironically Sierra Leone was established as a British naval base in 1807 to help prevent the prolific trade in human slaves shipped off from West Africa to the four corners of the earth.

By all accounts, the British had a tough time curtailing the flow of human cargo. Many observers complained that the local people were simply too pleasant and amenable, making them perfect fodder for coldhearted slavers seeking out suitable humans to trade for cash.

Now, almost 200 years later, that illicit trade still flourishes.

*   *   *

Little nine-year-old Hawa Kamara lived with her mother and six brothers and sisters in a simple, wooden shanty with a corrugated iron roof and a few beams to hold it up in Wilkinson Road, Freetown. As with most African families, the cooking was always done outside on a campfire. Water was obtained from a nearby well and toilet facilities consisted of a ditch at the back of the house.

Hawa's mother Yaya had always struggled to bring up the children; two other sons had died in infancy. Her husband was killed in a road accident just before Hawa's seventh birthday.

Yaya barely scraped a living together by growing vegetables on a small plot behind the house. She also obtained rice for the family from her brother in exchange for her help during the harvest time at his field 80 miles east of Freetown. But that was a risky venture as it involved leaving the children in the care of Hawa.

So when a Lebanese trader befriended the family they were most grateful. Every now and then he would appear at the shack with small gifts of milk and sometimes even meat for Yaya and her brood. They never once questioned his motives. That simply was not the way their minds worked.

The trader was a well-known figure in the bustling commercial center of Freetown, where he owned numerous clothing and jewelry stores, along with thousands of other Lebanese traders who settled in

Sierra Leone following the outbreak of war in their home country.

But one day the 52-year-old Arab appeared at the entrance to the shack bearing more gifts for Yaya and her children with a very blatant ulterior motive.

"It is time you let me give Hawa a good home away from all this," he explained patiently to Yaya. Then he produced a contract. It read:

AN AGREEMENT MADE THE 27TH DAY OF SEPTEMBER 1980 BETWEEN M. NASAAR, 28 EAST ST., FREETOWN N. SIERRA LEONE (HEREAFTER CALLED THE EM-PLOYER) AND DA MENDE KAMARA OF 151 WILKIN-SON RD., FREETOWN, SIERRA LEONE.
WHEREAS HAWA KAMARA IS IN THE EMPLOY-MENT OF THE EMPLOYER AS A HOUSEMAID AND IN THE COURSE OF HER EMPLOYMENT IS RE-QUESTED TO TRAVEL TO THE LEBANON.

The trader had signed the contract himself. Hawa's uncle had already been approached by the Arab and left his thumbprint because he could not write, and Hawa herself would later manage an almost illegible scrawl as her signature.

(Life expectancy in Sierra Leone has remained the lowest of any country in the world, according to the World Health Organization. A person can only expect to live an average of 41 years compared with well over 70 years of age in Britain and the United States. In these conditions, where life is so cheap, one less mouth to feed could mean the survival of the rest of the family.)

Like any good mother, Yaya wanted only what was best for her daughter. She looked around at the mud-encrusted shack and knew there had to be a better life for Hawa elsewhere, even if it meant separating her from her loved ones.

The trader then went on to explain to Yaya that he ''represented'' some other Lebanese traders who had returned to Beirut and wanted Hawa to work for them. The little girl sat just outside the entrance to the shack and listened intently to every word he was saying. She was confused. She had heard of many young girls who had gone to work for rich foreigners and never returned to their families. It had always been presumed that they had gone to live a better life away from the poverty of the slums. This was an opportunity to escape the misery, but it also might mean never seeing her family again.

Hawa started quietly sobbing as she contemplated the future without her family. Her mother had warned her that this day might come; she had tried to explain to Hawa that there simply was not enough food for the entire family. This was, in the words of her mother, a golden opportunity.

''Hawa, come here and talk to the gentleman,'' said Yaya, snapping the young girl out of her thoughts and back to reality.

Hawa got up and walked into the shack. The Lebanese turned towards her, a greasy smile across his face.

"You are going to nice people. They will look after you well and send you to school." He hesitated at that moment, then looked across at Yaya, who had an expectant expression on her face. "They will pay you every month and I will pass the money on to your mother."

Yaya looked quietly satisfied. She had been desperately looking for a means to increase her minimal income, and her nine-year-old daughter was about to provide it.

Hawa put her only belongings in a plastic shopping bag and then ran to the trader's Mercedes waiting in the muddy, washed-out track that ran in front of the shack. A few moments later, as the car pulled away, she wondered if she would ever see her family again.

Some hours later, Hawa was sitting in one of those big white birds that flew low over her shanty town every day as it taxied to the start of the runway. There was nothing she could do to prevent herself from being sent to Beirut. She was just nine years old. She had to trust Nasaar and hope that everything would turn out okay.

When the plane touched down in Beirut, a driver was waiting to whisk her off to an apartment block in Verdun Street, in the Muslim west side of the city. The house belonged to a local policeman, Muhammed Mahtoub and his wife Meisa. They were Hawa's master and mistress. Hawa was never formally introduced to them, but she was completely awed by the vast apartment the moment she stepped into it.

This was beautiful! Hawa dropped her belongings and ran over to the windows to look out and down at the street below. She had never experienced a view like this before. She turned into the room to look around. Woven rugs lay scattered across the pale, polished wooden floor, and even the furniture was arranged so that no one needed to sit with their backs toward the scenery. Natural canvas and heavy Muslim artifacts dominated the decor. A desk stood in the corner opposite the windows; natural light poured in. Hawa looked in wonderment at the antique painted pottery on the shelves of a glass-fronted cabinet; framed photos on one wall showed her master and mistress and their children.

It was only as Hawa was being told by the other servants never to use the same cutlery as the family who now owned her, that she even learned the name of her employers.

Hawa was given her own plate, fork, knife, and cup. She looked bewildered. Less than a day earlier, she had been living with her mother and brothers and sisters in a virtual mud hut. Just thinking about them made her burst into tears. She was a nine-year-old girl in a strange country without a friend or relative.

"Stop crying, girl!" screeched a voice from the front door area.

There was not a hint of humanity in Meisa Mahtoub's voice when she saw little Hawa sobbing.

"You cannot go home. You must stay here and work for us. We own you."

If Hawa had been a little older she might have appreciated the full meaning of those words. But as it was she had just begun a sentence as a slave that would go on for many, many years.

"There are no schools for black people in Beirut. You stay here. You do not go out. Do you understand?"

Hawa nodded her head as Meisa yelled at her yet again, just a few days after her arrival in Beirut. She had dared to ask about the trader's promise of education. Now she realized there was no point in pursuing the subject. The only things she was going to be taught involved housework, preparing food, and waiting at the table.

Soon Hawa was cooking for as many as 30 people whenever the Mahtoubs held dinner parties. She worked every day from 6:00 A.M. to midnight, sometimes even later if the family felt like staying up.

Hawa frequently fell asleep in her food, which usually consisted of scraps of leftovers. She was forbidden from eating until everything in the house had been cleared up. Often the food consisted of hard crusts of bread and regurgitated meat spat out onto the plate by one of the Mahtoub's guests.

Humiliation was a popular pastime for Meisa and her husband. When little Hawa did not clear the plates fast enough or cook the food on time, they would grab her by the hair and tell her, "Faster! Slave! Faster! What have you been doing?"

Sometimes, when she was just serving her master and mistress, Hawa would be made to crawl on all fours across the floor before getting up and clearing the table. Meisa told the child that neither she or her husband wanted to look at her face. Later, Hawa concluded that whenever they saw her eyes it made them feel guilty about their abuse of her.

One day, Hawa spilled some soup on the marble floor of the dining room. Muhammed Mahtoub exploded as his wife looked on contentedly.

"Dog! Clear it up! Now!"

Hawa was frozen to the spot with fear. But her lack of movement was interpreted as defiance by the policeman. He grabbed her by the wrist and pushed her over his lap. Then she felt the leather sole of his shoe beating her.

At the other end of the table Meisa watched, licking her lips with cold satisfaction.

As Muhammed continued beating the child, she felt his other hand sliding between her legs. She struggled in response, but he just beat her harder, and his fingers probed even deeper.

"Maybe we should just kill her?" Meisa said coldly from her vantage point.

"No. That would be too good for her."

At that moment, Muhammed removed the belt from his trousers and pushed Hawa forward over the dining room table before beating her at least a dozen more times.

That night, Hawa cried herself to sleep. She was so confused. Anything, even life back in the slums, had to be better than this.

* * *

"Please! Please let me out of here!"

The screams and moans coming from the closet beneath the stairs echoed around the house. But no one took any notice. The mistress of the house had insisted on stuffing towels underneath the door to the closet so that it muffled Hawa's cries for help. No one seemed to care about her. She was completely on her own.

Hawa strained her ears to listen for any telltale signs of what was happening outside that cupboard. She'd been in there for more than one day when the heat became so intense that she'd desperately peeled off her few clothes. It was almost 100 degrees. The air became even more musty and thick as the temperature rose.

On the third day of Hawa's incarceration, she heard someone at the entrance to the closet. It sounded as if they were about to unlock it. But then whoever it was walked away. She began to believe she would never see daylight again.

She found herself focusing on something long and brown, with a brush on the end of it . . . the broom. It was the only other thing inside the closet with her.

She'd been banished from sleeping in the tiny room they called a bedroom. Instead she'd been forced into this tiny closet. Hawa sobbed inside that dreadful prison. The tears ran down her face and smudged the dust that now covered her entire body. Then she noticed a tiny sliver of light above through a crack in the boards of the closet. She leaned towards it and tried to inhale the outside air in the hope it might revive her flagging body. But as she desperately sucked at the tiny hole her head began to spin. Hawa fell down and hit her head on a sharp nail protruding from the inside of the locked closet door.

On the filthy floor she tried to breathe in the clean air that she'd snatched at moments earlier, but her throat was filled with dustballs. She started to choke. She couldn't breathe. It was if she were drowning.

Suddenly, Hawa's eyes burst open and she felt the bruises on the side of her body. She'd just had a terrible nightmare, but the reality of life was no better.

Hawa's ordinary domestic chores shrank into insignificance once Muhammed and his wife stepped up the number of beatings she received. As the only full-time servant in the Mahtoub's four-bedroom apartment, there were many things to do every day. She had to struggle out to the veranda with a huge carpet, which then had to have every speck of dust beaten out of it. Then she had to water every one of the hundreds of plants scattered around the apartment. Meisa had warned Hawa that if any of them died then she would be beaten severely. Hawa was even expected to wash every single leaf.

Then there were the mirrors, windows, and floors that had to be polished to perfection. Hawa found herself praying to God every night that she would not get sick because the Mahtoubs would never allow her to see a doctor, let alone take time off if she felt unwell.

After more than a year as a slave to the Mahtoubs, Hawa felt the emotion begin to drain out of her mind and body. In those first 12 months she had cried so much that it was starting to get difficult to shed any more tears. She had learned how to repress her true emotions for fear that the Mahtoubs might see her and then they would beat her.

The worst attack of all had occurred when Muhammed had arrived home drunk after a police function. His wife was away visiting relatives and he was so incapable he could not open the front door with his key. When Hawa answered it, his face lit up with depraved lust.

"Why did you take so long, dog?"

Hawa did not answer. She knew that to reply would seem insolent. She did not want to make things any worse for herself.

As she closed the door behind the sweating, overweight Muhammed, she smelled the pungent aroma of alcohol on his breath. She turned to walk towards her tiny bedroom when he caught her wrist and swung her around, crushing her slight body against his.

"Talk, dog. Say something!"

"Yes, master," was about all poor little Hawa could reply. She was shaking with fear, horribly aware of what might be about to follow.

Suddenly, Muhammed took a clump of her hair in his other hand and began dragging the girl along the hallway floor. Hawa did not utter another sound that night. She just stared at the ceiling once they got to his bedroom and tried to think of the better life she was sure existed somewhere outside the prison she inhabited.

But Hawa couldn't really think straight; she didn't dare think. Every word that animal said, the images it invoked, the incredible humiliation of it all was too overwhelming.

The fear, the pain. When would it ever end? Hawa dared not think about getting her freedom one day. She now believed it would never happen. Whenever she tried to think of the good times in the past it just made it worse. Remembering her family and the few special moments in her short life increased the suffering.

This was a living nightmare.

The following days consisted of one beating after another. Each one worse than the previous. Muhammed forced Hawa to do everything he demanded—there were no exceptions to the rule. She rose before dawn to clean the apartment, and that was just the beginning. It seemed as if every inch of the apartment had to be cleaned over and over again. In the evening Hawa was banished from going to bed. She was never once asked about her feelings. She was treated just like the dirt she was made to clean. Even with all the chores completed, Hawa was expected to stand to attention in a corner of the room ready to carry out any of her master's wishes. He seemed obsessed with making sure that if his wife got home then she would walk into an apartment that was truly immaculate. Hawa's right hand soon ached with an intense pain that would never go away.

Muhammed seemed determined to cause Hawa the maximum amount of suffering. When she disobeyed, she was beaten with anything that he could lay his hands on. Just walking had become agony and she knew it was going to get even worse. Not a moment passed when she did not feel the pain searing through her body. Her feelings were numbing. Everything was a daze. Nothing mattered anymore.

On the second night he chained her to the end of his bed like some rabid dog and at regular intervals unlocked the padlock and forced her to perform. For the first time in her miserable life, Hawa actually prayed to be locked up because at least that meant he would leave her alone.

On the last morning before the mistress arrived home, Hawa was unchained and told to get to work. She soon became aware of Muhammed following her from room to room, his eyes bearing down on her from every angle.

"Do not tell anyone about this," he cautioned her. "Do not breathe a word about what has happened."

He looked her in the eye one last time before he left her to continue with her chores.

"If you embarrass me," he whispered, trailing one finger down between her breasts, "I'll kill you. Do you understand?"

"Yes, sir," she whispered back. Trembling seemed about to overtake her entire body, but she gritted her teeth together, determined not to show him the full extent of her fear.

*　　*　　*

Hawa was never allowed out of the Beirut apartment except to walk across the street to the bakery for some bread. But her occasional tastes of freedom proved almost as unpleasant as her life behind the closed doors of the Mahtoub household.

As she skipped across the street to the bakery, local children and adults would hurl racial insults in her direction. They liked to call her "chocolate" and shouted Arabic words meaning banana and watermelon.

The second time she went to the bakery, a rock hit her on the head. She turned to look where it had come from and saw a man in his twenties sneering towards her.

"Nigger girl. Go home!"

If only I could, thought Hawa. I would give anything to get out of this devil's playground and return to the shantytown.

Just then, another three rocks showered down on her. She knew she could not return to the apartment empty-handed because the Mahtoubs would beat her for failing in her duties. Hawa heard gunfire and explosions in the distance as the war in Beirut was still raging. But her only battle at that time was to survive.

As the months turned into years, Hawa started to experience a disturbing loss in the track of time. She was banned from seeing anything that might actually tell her what the date was, even the correct year. After a couple of years, she stopped celebrating her birthday because she did not know when it was and nobody seemed to care.

She no longer even knew her own age. She was never taught to read or write. She was living a highly restricted life within four walls in a city she had only briefly glimpsed from the airport all those years previously.

Hawa did manage to make a slight friend of Vera, another girl from Sierra Leone who also worked as a slave for another Lebanese family in the same apartment block. But both girls were extremely careful not to allow their respective families to find out because they knew they would be punished.

Unable to write, Hawa called on Vera to write letters to her family back in Freetown. But she never received any replies, apart from two letters which were sent via Vera. Hawa started to suspect that whenever she left out letters for the postman, the Mahtoubs would simply destroy them when she was not looking.

Then in 1985, at the age of 15, Hawa suddenly found herself being bundled off to the Beirut airport to be flown back to Freetown. The teenager was confused. The Mahtoubs had always told her that she belonged to them and would not ever be able to go home. Now, for no apparent reason, she was about to have her dream come true. Or was she?

Meisa Mahtoub told Hawa that she was being taken back to Sierra Leone to renew her passport. Since the document had been confiscated from her the moment she arrived in Beirut, Hawa had no idea she even had one in the first place.

But Hawa's face dropped when she was met at Freetown airport by the same Lebanese trader, the man who was responsible for all the misery she had endured over the previous years. He took her arm and guided her to his Mercedes. Hawa, more assertive than before, tried to fathom out from the Arab what was happening. She wanted to know if she could stay in Freetown. She certainly never wanted to go back to that apartment in Beirut ever again.

"I want the money that you promised to pay my family. I know you have never given it to them," she told him.

The Arab raised his hands in surrender.

"Of course. I made a contract, and I have no intention of breaking that agreement.'

Hawa was mildly surprised. She had expected him to try and avoid paying any of the money owed to her and her family. He seemed to be acting in an honorable manner.

He pulled out his wallet and counted out $65.

"There you are."

Hawa looked down at the money in disgust.

"What is this? You owe my family much more than that. I have been away for years."

The problem was that Hawa did not actually know how long she had been away. She thought it was a couple of years but she could not be sure.

"I'll pay your mother the rest of the money when you go back to Beirut."

Hawa was stunned by what she was hearing. She had no intention of returning to that city.

"But . . . I am home now."

The trader completely ignored Hawa and continued.

"Your mother needs this money very badly. I am offering to pay her the entire amount on condition you go back to Beirut. You have no choice."

"But my family is here."

"Your family don't need you here, but they do need your money."

Hawa sank into the seat in the back of his Mercedes. She was caught. Nowhere to turn. She could not quite believe that she was back in her hometown but unable to stay. She pleaded with him to let her remain a few days with her mother.

"Okay. But you must go back to Beirut when I say."

Hawa agreed, although she secretly hoped that she could reverse the situation. She just needed a bit of time. But one problem Hawa did not allow for was her mother.

Yaya made it clear from the moment her daughter arrived at that old familiar shack on the outskirts of the city that she did not want Hawa around. Yaya saw the now-shapely teenager as a threat to the peace and tranquility of her home. Local men kept calling round at the hut after hearing about how Hawa had blossomed into an attractive young woman. Yaya felt threatened. She was used to being the only adult female in the household. In any case, she wanted Hawa to get back to Beirut to earn the remainder of that money the trader had promised.

One night, Hawa even sat down with her mother after the other children had gone to bed and tried to explain how awful her life in Beirut had been. But Yaya closed her ears to it all. She believed that Hawa was lying. How could life be that bad in such a civilized country?

Within hours of Hawa getting her new passport, the trader was taking her back to the airport to get on that plane. If anything, she felt even more demoralized than the last time she made the trip because now not even her mother seemed prepared to offer her true love and affection.

When Hawa arrived back in Beirut, she found that the civil war had intensified and the large apartment block where the Mahtoubs lived was regularly caught in the crossfire. During this period many Arab families left the city, but Muhammed Mahtoub—now a captain in the Muslim forces—insisted his family remain.

As the bombs and sniper fire rained down on them, the Mahtoubs decided that life might be safer if they moved to the shelters built in the basement of the block. They left Hawa to live in the apartment on her own.

''We don't want the black slave too close to us,'' she overheard Meisa telling her husband. Hawa also believed that Meisa did not want her to have any opportunity to be alone with her husband. Just before they evacuated, Meisa had pulled Hawa aside and warned her to keep away from Muhammed "unless I am in the room."

So, with bombs and snipers constantly pounding the building, Hawa was left all alone while the Mahtoubs lived in comparative safety downstairs in the basement.

Frequently, she found herself cowering in the passageway in the middle of the apartment while bullets whistled through the windows, some of them of such high velocity that they pierced the plaster walls.

One time, she crawled on her hands and knees to the front door as explosions ripped all around her. Gasping for breath, she pulled open the door only to be confronted by a hooded gunman spraying his machine gun in the ceiling of the hallway.

"Get back! Get back!" he screamed at her. She slammed the door shut and sat huddled in a corner praying that he would not burst into the apartment. She does not know to this day why he did not kill her.

But the worst aspect of being in that apartment during the attacks was the loneliness. It wasn't as if she enjoyed the company of the Mahtoubs, but she did feel that there was some safety in numbers.

Sometimes Hawa, still only 15 years old, was so frightened that she could not stop shaking. On at least one occasion she found herself so paralyzed with fear that she urinated on the spot where she crouched from the warring factors blasting away just outside the building. When the bombing subsided that day, she was just as frightened that the Mahtoubs would return to the apartment and discover what she had done.

After months of enduring the relentless bombardments, Hawa started to believe that perhaps she would be better off dead. One time, as blasts shook the very foundations of the apartment block, Hawa walked onto the balcony of the building and started talking to herself.

"Let them kill me! My life is nothing. I would be better off dead."

As Hawa stood there, she saw a number of people killed in the street below. She felt a wave of envy for them. At least their last battle was over. She watched as a man was stabbed to death by another in the gutter following ferocious hand-to-hand combat.

Then Hawa leaned over the balcony to see a man three stories below her level. He had something in his hand. It might have been a grenade or maybe a cluster bomb. Just then, another man appeared with a rifle moving swiftly across the street below. At that moment the man on the balcony dropped the bomb directly onto the man's head. It exploded on impact, decapitating the man.

In the middle of all this carnage, Hawa's mistress Meisa would telephone her from the family's basement hideaway demanding that she bring them food and drinks.

"And make it quick. We are very hungry and thirsty," Meisa told her young slave girl, conveniently ignoring the bombs and bullets.

Hawa did not dare point out the obvious; that she would be risking her life by leaving the apartment at that particular moment. Instead she replaced the receiver and started to prepare the food. A short while later, she struggled along the hallway of the apartment with the food on a tray before scrambling down the many flights of steps to the basement.

Meisa was not exactly grateful.

"Next time make more. We get very hungry down here."

As Hawa turned to leave, Meisa remembered something else.

"And don't forget to clean the apartment of all the broken glass before we come back."

During a break in fighting a few months later, Meisa called Hawa into the living room. Her beautiful, blonde 23-year-old daughter Anila was there. Hawa had long since despised this girl with her designer-label clothes and sneering expression. When she was a teenager, Anila had been ruthless and cruel to Hawa, taunting her about her race and even the size of her breasts.

"I have a new job for you,' said Meisa. 'From now on you are slave to Anila."

Hawa said nothing. But then Anila spoke.

"Thank you, Mommy. Thank you so much. She is the best wedding present I could ever hope for."

It was only then that Hawa realized she had been

given to Anila as a gift for her forthcoming wedding. Within weeks, Hawa was on her way to a new country with her young, arrogant mistress. When the young girl had heard it was London, the capital city of Britain, she felt that perhaps her nightmare might be slowly coming to an end. Surely there was no way that Anila could keep her as a slave in such a civilized society? Slavery was outlawed in places like London. Or so Hawa thought.

But the drudgery worsened in London. The family lived in a vast mansion on St. John's Wood Road, just a stone's throw from Regent's Park. Hawa found herself working as maid, cook, butler, and nanny to Anila's baby. Her hours started before five every morning and never ended before midnight. It was a relentless, seven-days-a-week existence and she never once received a penny in wages.

By the end of 1986, Hawa was in her seventh year of slavery. She could not read or write. She was terrified to go out of the house because Anila had told her there were rapists and murderers on every street corner. The windows to the house were barred, and a sophisticated alarm system was tripped the moment anyone tried to enter or leave the premises. At night, private security guards patrolled every two hours in the grounds. It was a fortress in the middle of a country that Hawa thought was a bastion of freedom—until she had arrived there.

Whenever Anila left the house, she went to enormous lengths to lock Hawa in. Her initial promises of providing Hawa with some form of education were rapidly forgotten.

The family had a BMW, a Mercedes, and a Bentley in the driveway, but they never once offered to pay for anything for Hawa, let alone hand over the salary that had been due since that day in Freetown when the trader had made his offer to Hawa's family.

With absolutely nothing to lose, Hawa began to try and persuade the hard-nosed Anila to let her attend some sort of schooling in London. Finally, after months of requests, Anila arranged for Hawa to go to English classes for just one hour a week. She was to be accompanied by the family's chauffeur, who would take her directly home once the class had finished.

Hawa found it so strange being out in the big, wide world. She felt extremely nervous and wary of talking to anyone, especially after the ominous warning given to her by Anila just after they arrived in London.

In the classroom, Hawa had great difficulty concentrating because she was so scared of being out on her own. It has to be remembered that she had not been given this much freedom since those far-off days in the slums of Freetown.

"What is the matter, Hawa?" asked her teacher one day.

The teenager was too frightened to respond.

"Nothing, sir," was all she could say.

Hawa considered telling her teacher the truth about her awful life of slavery. But then she remembered what Anila told her just before she started school.

"Don't even think about telling anyone about your life here because if you lose this job, the police will throw you out of the country. You will get into a lot of trouble. Maybe you will even be killed."

Hawa's teacher repeated the question. "Are you sure there is nothing wrong?"

Hawa shivered with fear and trepidation. She just dared not say anything.

That afternoon, Hawa's teacher rang Anila to ask her why Hawa had been acting so strangely. It was a caring thought on the part of the teacher, but unfortunately it sparked a tirade of further abuse for the young girl.

After just four lessons, Anila forbade Hawa to go to school any more. "You cannot be trusted. You will stay here all the time," was her explanation to Hawa.

The only aspect of Hawa's life that was any more bearable in London was that at least she did not have to contend with the lecherous Muhammed Mahtoub forcing her to have sex.

Hawa even befriended a West Indian woman called Mary Apple, who came in to help with the cleaning of the vast house and struck up conversations with Hawa despite Anila's obvious disapproval.

The young, blonde wife deliberately forced her two servants to work at opposite ends of the house so that it would be virtually impossible for them to communicate. But Mary had recognized in Hawa a needy soul from the moment they met, and she was determined to get to the know the young woman.

Whenever Anila went to the gym for a workout or disappeared to the beautician or hairdresser, Mary would seek out Hawa and talk to her. Sometimes they would chat together for hours. Mary gradually pieced together Hawa's sad and tragic life as a slave girl.

Mary was shocked when she discovered that not only did Hawa's workday start earlier and end much later than hers, but she had never once been paid. And when Hawa told her that she was not allowed out of the house, even to walk as far as the wrought-iron gates at the end of the driveway, Mary became even more determined to help the young girl.

She invited Hawa to stay at her home for Christmas that year because she could not stand the thought of that poor girl remaining all alone in the house on such a festive occasion.

But Anila and her husband soon put a stop to such plans.

"You will stay here. You will never leave the house," the young wife told her slave. "Remember what I told you. If you disobey us you will be thrown out of the country."

Hawa did not argue with her mistress.

"You will do exactly as I say. If you dare to argue with me I will beat you even more. You are our servant and you have no voice. Your opinion means nothing. Is that clear?"

That evening Anila beat Hawa black and blue with

a horsewhip when she failed to close the door behind her after she had served her mistress her supper in the living room.

Hawa did not utter a word as Mary sponged hot and cold water over her body. She gave her a cup of tea to warm her. She drank it down virtually in one gulp.

Mary laughed dryly as she accepted the young girl's apologies about why she had to work that Christmas and could not visit her home. Through the pain of that thrashing, Hawa was still worrying about upsetting her only friend. It was a touching gesture.

As Mary helped Hawa get dressed, she was seething at the treatment meted out to her young friend. She was further infuriated when she discovered that many of the letters she had written for Hawa to her family were being thrown away by Anila before they could be posted.

Worse still, only a handful of letters from Hawa's family in West Africa were given to Hawa, which also could only mean one thing: that Anila was throwing them away as well.

Mary advised Hawa to try and get to the front door for the post before Anila every morning because she would probably never hand over the letters from Hawa's family. It had become crystal clear to Mary that Hawa was being treated appallingly. She begged her young friend to consider running away but those threats from Anila were constantly ringing in Hawa's ears. She was also terrified of what life would be like in the world outside.

The unhappiness was filling her entire day. She had thought there was always hope, but now that had all gone. She began to blame herself. Maybe it was all her own fault?

When Mary decided to leave Anila's employment to take on another, better-paid job, Hawa was very saddened because Mary had become her only real contact with the world beyond those four walls.

But Mary had already decided that, with nothing to lose, she was going to help Hawa escape. She began to plan a clever scheme that she believed was completely foolproof. It involved persuading Anila to take on Mary's sister, Denise, as a part-time cleaner while she was looking for a new employee.

Denise was more than happy to play a role in the scheme once she had been told of Hawa's plight. The two women sat Hawa down one day and explained in detail how they were going to bring her enslavement to an end after so many tortuous years.

A few days later the plan was put into operation. Denise made an excuse to Anila as to why she had to stay late to finish polishing the silver in the dining room. This would mean Anila would have to leave the house without locking the front door from the outside, as she always did whenever she left Hawa alone in the property.

Within minutes of Anila departing, Denise helped

Hawa pack her few belongings and they left that house. Minutes later they caught a taxi to Mary's home five miles away in North London. It had been a remarkably simple plan to execute. But Hawa's problems were only just beginning.

It took two months of wrangling between police, social workers, and the Lebanese family to get them to return Hawa's passport to her. When Hawa finally saw it, she learned that her birthday was on October 4. According to the passport, she was born in 1968 and so was 19 years old when she ran away from the family in 1987. She actually believed she was only 16.

And her freedom also brought with it many more, fresh problems. While enslaved in one of London's smartest areas, she had painstakingly learned to write her name, but could write little more. She had never been on a bus or the subway, and had never even walked down a London street. She was alone in London apart from Mary Apple. She had no money, nowhere to live, and no legal right to reside in Britain. She did not want to return to Freetown because she knew her mother could not afford to keep her.

Eventually, after months more of legal wrangling, Hawa won the right to stay in Britain. She is now working and living with an English family in the London area. She still remains very frightened of the outside world.

''I am just as scared now because I have no right

place to live. No home, no country. If anything happens to me, no one knows where I am,'' Hawa says.

Neither the Mahtoubs nor the man who originally sold Hawa into slavery have ever been brought to justice for enslaving her for almost half her life.

20

VIOLA

A slave must be intelligent, truthful, unique, and loyal. Most of all she must have the time to prove herself to me.
        Mistress Mir (1996)

———

TWO-STORY HOUSE, TREE-LINED STREET, NEW JERSEY, JANUARY, 1996

5:45 A.M.: The ear-piercing noise of the alarm clock was long and loud. Viola snapped open her eyes and tried with difficulty to move in her narrow single bed because skintight black leather restraints were digging into her wrists and ankles. But she did not dare to utter a word in case her mistress got angry. Yet another long and gruelling day as the ultimate slave was about to begin.

Viola had lain there trapped for eight hours following an evening at the hands of her employer.

But unlike any other slave, Viola was not eaten up with fear and loathing for her mistress. Instead, she felt a surge of excitement flow through her body as she thought about the brutal regime that she faced that and every day.

Two hours later, the door swung open and her mistress, a striking, glamorous African-American woman called Mir, strode into the room. Viola looked up and then shut her eyes tightly as her mistress slapped her across her face.

A few minutes later, Viola's wrists and ankles were unshackled. She stretched her body as she got out of bed and adjusted the leather collar round her neck which represented yet more evidence of her enslavement. Viola enjoyed wearing the collar because it reminded her of her adoration for her mistress Mir, the woman to whom she had become utterly devoted over the previous two years.

Incredibly, amongst the millions of women slaves still in existence today, there are estimated to be tens of thousands of voluntary slaves who've allowed themselves to become full-time devotees to men and women masters.

There is something remarkably ironic about this phenomenon, which is growing at an alarming pace throughout the so-called civilized world. It is almost as if the appalling degradation of innocent women has incited the more twisted members of society to become embroiled in sexual perversity that features the brutality that most societies are trying their hardest to stamp out.

Viola is a classic example: She lives as a full-time slave to a beautiful woman in a quiet suburban New

Jersey neighborhood in the heart of classic middle Americana.

Behind the closed doors of a beautifully decorated house worth many hundreds of thousands of dollars, Viola allows herself to be abused and beaten and humiliated all in the name of her love for her mistress.

Viola even has Mir's name tattooed on her leg as a permanent reminder of her enslavement to her mistress.

She explains in deadly serious tones, "I am her property. She can do what she wants to me. I have given my life to her."

Viola's route to sexual enslavement is extraordinary because outwardly she seems more like a friendly, middle-aged housewife. But behind her calm demeanor and warm sense of humor lies a woman who has felt the need to offer herself completely and utterly to a mistress.

Up until her incarceration, she had suffered abuse at the hands of uncaring, disloyal men in a string of disastrous relationships. Yet that enforced violence has driven her into the arms of a relationship in which pain is the key word.

Viola's own sick and elderly mother encouraged her to become a full-time slave to mistress Mir, who was an old family friend.

"My mother was very seriously ill in the hospital but she sensed that I needed to be controlled and looked after by someone who really cared. She actually picked Mir for me. She understood my weaknesses and considered that Mir would actually improve the quality and happiness in my life,'' Viola says.

Just hours after meeting Mir at her mother's hospital bedside, Viola and her mistress-to-be returned to Mir's dungeon where Viola happily became a slave to her every whim and desire.

''From that day on, I realized, whenever Mir showed up at the hospital, my mom lit up. Whenever Mir wasn't around, Mom was talking about Mir. She encouraged us.''

Viola speaks about her enslavement as if it was the most normal event in the world. ''I am a genuine S&M pervert and being a slave helps me to chase my fantasies. I feel no shame.''

At the age of 44, Viola says she feels that her enslavement is more than just another example of sexual perversity. ''I live every aspect of my life as a slave. I feel no guilt because this is what I want.''

Part of that devotion to mistress Mir entails being ''lent out'' to other mistresses if Mir commands it.

''Viola is my property,'' says Mir. ''If I decide that she should be tortured by others then it is entirely up to me.''

Mir explains her role as a mistress with pleasurable detachment.

''Being a dominant gives me assumed control in most situations. These are not privileges that I use with indifference.''

Those ''privileges'' include bondage, fetishes, feminization, and role-playing. Says Mir, ''Equestrian scenes, military scenes, medical scenes, and historical scenes are just a few of the role-playing scenes that I get into. I enjoy becoming the character that I play.''

Mir openly admits to using a favorite instrument of torture on Viola and the other part-time slaves that sometimes visit her home. ''It is a four-foot single-tailed signal whip. I love to use it because of the amount of control and skill the whip requires.''

She even insists, ''I can swing the whip with my full strength and still not cause harm.''

And Mir's slave Viola is no simple country girl trapped into a life of degradation. She has a bachelor's degree in teaching and insists that her life is the one she has chosen.

But there have been a few close shaves along the way as she has encountered other dominants whose demands are not quite as reasonable as those of her mistress Mir.

One time a male dominant to whom Mir loaned Viola forced a needle filled with high-grade heroin into Viola's backside. She lost consciousness and then had to go ''cold turkey'' for a week to recover from the massive dose of narcotics.

Another time she was almost suffocated during a dangerous bout of sexual activity and some of the beatings she has suffered have certainly scarred her for life.

But Viola is unrepentant. ''This is the life I have chosen. My mistress Mir ultimately controls every aspect of my life. This is the way I want it to be. Many people will find it hard to understand what I am and certainly enforced enslavement is something that should only occur on a voluntary basis.''

Remarkably, 90 percent of Viola's typical day as a slave to mistress Mir sounds very mundane.

''I make her breakfast, accompany her to appointments, pick up her children from school, help them with their homework, cook everyone supper, and keep the house in good order,'' she explains earnestly. ''I am her friend, bodyguard, assistant, lover, slave.''

At around midnight almost every evening, Viola's apparently ordinary existence turns into something far more disturbing.

''That's when madam decides it is time for danger, which means severe physical punishment is likely to occur,'' explains Viola.

That punishment usually involves a visit to mistress Mir's dungeon, or ''playroom,'' as she calls it.

The array of torture instruments that line the walls of this plushly carpeted room include:

- Five closets where mistress Mir often locks Viola or any of her other part-time slaves for hours on end
- A huge wooden cross where slaves are often left
- Iron cages
- Swings from the ceiling
- A king-size leather four-post bed complete with built-in wrist and ankle restraints
- A medieval-style rack
- A throne where Mir often sits before barking orders to her slaves
- A coffin where some slaves are forced to lie

"That playroom represents a heightened state of craziness when slaves like me are in the mood to be punished," explains Viola.

And Mir positively beams with pride when talking about her playroom.

"I'm very proud of it. Everything in it was custom-made for me. It is the dream dungeon. Many of the major pieces of bondage furniture in my playroom are works of art.

"The inquisitor's chair is copied from one I saw in a medieval museum of torture. The coffin was inspired by a trip I made to Egypt. The roasting chair was modeled after a chair used by witch hunters to force confessions by roasting the genitals of the person strapped to it."

Three or four times a year, Viola's mistress Mir hosts parties at her rambling house that last for two days and "where anything goes."

But probably one of the most bizarre aspects of Viola's weird lifestyle as a sexual slave is that she was recently the victim of a kidnap attempt by a millionaire African businessman.

"This guy decided that he wanted to take me back to Africa and keep me forever but I wanted to stay with Mir," explains Viola.

After many weeks of negotiation, the businessman eventually abandoned his plans to snatch Viola.

But then last year, a wealthy diplomat at the United Nations in New York offered Mir half a million dollars to "buy" Viola and turn her into his full-time slave.

Once again, her devotion to her current mistress took precedence and the offer was politely declined.

Viola adds, "It was very flattering, but I am happy living and working for Mir. I don't want any other master or mistress."

Her mistress says that while there is inevitably a level of humiliation involved in how she treats slave Viola, "humiliation differs from person to person. There are too many shades of gray to this topic for me to say whether or not I can, or will, humiliate anyone.

"My personal code of ethics is simple. I treat my slaves with respect. They are all valued for their individuality. I will do nothing that would jeopardize myself or the well-being of my slave."

And Viola's devotion to her mistress is unquestionable.

"Madam is an incredible woman. And by God's good grace, we'll never be apart from each other again."

APPENDIX

FURTHER CASES

It is not the whip that makes men, but the lure of things that are worthy to be loved.
Woodrow Wilson (1906)

———

In addition to the cases already described in vivid detail in *Slave Girls*, these examples provide even further evidence that, as we rapidly approach the next century, the enslavement of women continues in many different forms.

United Arab Emirates

Case: Filipina maid Sarah Balabagan, 16, had her death sentence commuted to 100 lashes after stabbing to death a member of the household where she was enslaved. She was being raped at the time. (1995)

Britain

Case: Brett Mills, age 34, from Croydon, South London, imprisoned a 12-year-old girl in an apartment as his sex slave and then subjected her to an appalling series of attacks. He was found guilty of various sex crimes and imprisoned for 15 years. (1995)

Ghana

Case: Thousands of girls are being forced into menial and sexual slavery by being given away as *Tro-kasis* (the term means "fetish slave") to single men. Their families in remote villages believe they will improve a run of bad luck by allowing their children to be enslaved. (1995)

India

Case: Up to 50,000 Nepalese girls are believed to be currently enslaved in brothels in Bombay. Most of them are working to repay the price their families were paid for them. (1995)

Brazil

Case: Geralda Santos was held as a slave for two years in a town in the north of the country. She was made to sleep in the garden, given only one meal a day, and not allowed to keep her child with her. (1995)

Japan

Case: Former women prisoners of war finally gained some recognition for their plight during World War II when hundreds of them were set up as so-called "comfort women" in prison brothels controlled by the Japanese armed forces. The Japanese government agreed to consider compensation payments to the surviving women. (1995)

Pakistan

Case: Tens of thousands of workers are being held in various forms of slavery, according to the latest findings from the Human Rights Watch charity in Asia. The group says that women are being forced into slave labor camps to work as carpet-weavers. (1995)

Italy

Case: Maria-Rosario Rota, 31, was kept locked in a bedroom for 17 years by parents who thought the world too evil for her. She was found after a nun tipped off police in Colnago, Northern Italy. (1995)

United States

Case: Dayna Broussard, age eight, was beaten to death by members of a commune at their isolated farmhouse in Sandy, near Portland, Oregon. She had been kept enslaved along with 53 other children at the property. (1991)

United States

Case: Los Angeles businessman Nasim Mussry and his sister Elsa Singman, convicted in connection with selling 60 women into involuntary servitude to people who paid $3,000 each to use them as domestic servants. (1985)

Canada

Case: Paul Bernardo, an accountant, found guilty of murdering two schoolgirls whom he enslaved in his bungalow in St. Catherines, Ontario. He was convicted of nine charges, including first-degree murder, kidnappings, confinements, and rape. (1995)

South Africa

Case: Jabulile Masuka, age 17, was seriously assaulted by, the man who purchased her, as well as the agent who sold her, after she was secretly transported across the border from Mozambique to villages in the Komatipoort area of Eastern Transvaal. (1990)

Sierra Leone

Case: Adama Bangura was just 16 when her parents sold her to a businessman in Abidjan. She was then transported to Lebanon as a slave where she was trapped against her will for three years before finally escaping back to her home country. (1990)

Britain

Case: Ruthless madam Myra Ling-Ling Forde lured schoolgirls living in care into working as prostitutes for her and then trapped them against their will. She was eventually arrested and sentenced to six years in jail. (1995)

Britain

Case: Maria Gomez, 30, was brought to Britain by a Palestinian and his wife who forced her into a life of slavery. She finally escaped from their clutches but only after enduring beatings and verbal abuse and a wage of just two pounds a week. (1991)

Britain

Case: Anita Reyes had to escape from her employers by tying bedsheets together and climbing out of her second-floor bedroom window in the center of London. She had been regularly beaten by the wife of her employer. (1992)

Britain

Case: Lulu's employer was a British army major serving abroad in Brunei. She returned to Britain with the family. But she was ordered to sleep at the end of her master's bed whenever his wife was away visiting friends and relatives in the country and endured regular beatings and sexual abuse. She eventually escaped but was too frightened to press charges against the family. (1993)

United States

Case: Rima, just 19, endured severe beatings at the hand of her employer even after moving from Saudi Arabia to the glamorous city of Los Angeles. The beautiful Indian girl was threatened with death if she uttered a word about her enslavement. (1993)

Britain

Case: Cindy Dindial was slapped, kicked, punched, and beaten with a rolling pin while tied up, virtually every day of her employment, at the hands of two evil doctors in the historical English city of Lincoln. After six months of nonstop torture and abuse, Cindy courageously walked out with nothing but the clothes she stood in and went to the police. Both these evil doctors were jailed after being convicted of assault and causing actual bodily harm. It was a very rare case of prosecution as a result of a complaint by a slave domestic. (1993)

Kuwait/Britain

Case: For three years Alice Santos was abused by her Kuwaiti employers. She finally escaped when the family took her to London on a vacation. But she believes to this day that her life is in danger because she has dared to speak out against her former employers. (1992)

Switzerland

Case: Teresa worked in Kuwait as a domestic for relatives of the Al Sabah royal family. When news of the Iraqi invasion came, she was abandoned by her employers and taken back to the royal palace in Kuwait City. She eventually escaped to the family's home in Switzerland, where she was raped and beaten by one teenage prince. No action was ever taken against the family. (1991)

India

Case: Little Ameena Begum was sold by her father to a wealthy Arab sheik when she was just 10 years old. Sixty-year-old Yahya al-Sagish paid $4,000 and was then caught trying to smuggle little Ameena through an airport where he planned to board a jet for Saudi Arabia. It even transpired that al-Sagish had already "married" the little girl in a wedding ceremony in India and planned to use her as his sex slave for the rest of his life. After Ameena's arrest police discovered photographs of four other girls in his possession. It is understood he had a harem of women waiting for him back in Saudi Arabia. He was jailed for a year. (1991)

Nigeria/Britain

Case: Roseline Tigani, age 15, was sold for $3 to an English couple from Sheffield, in the north of England. Forced to work 18 hours a day as a servant and made to kneel at the foot of her master and mistress's bedroom door every night, Roseline eventually escaped, took her former employers to court and was awarded $30,000 in damages. However, the British Home Office deported her immediately after her court victory because she had illegally overstayed her visa. (1990)

Spain

Case: Sofia was taken from her village in southeast Spain to Valencia when she was just 12 years old and sold to a Lebanese family by her father in exchange for $50. Enslaved in Madrid, Sofia befriended a woman who persuaded her to run away. She started working as a prostitute to survive. But she still preferred life on the streets to life inside that demonic family. She is still working as a prostitute and her abusers have never been brought to justice. (1994)

Brazil

Case: Women slaves are being hired by the dozen in the Amazon frontier town of Maraba. Police occasionally raid ranches where they are being held captive, but there are rarely prosecutions of the offending land owners. (1990)

<u>Morocco</u>

Case: Girls as young as 12 are working grueling 55-hour weeks in sweltering temperatures in a factory in Meknes. Many of the garments produced end up on the shelves of some of Britain's best-known chain stores.

For sufferers it is sweet to know beforehand clearly the pain that remains for them.
    Aeschylus (470 B.C.)

————

Nothing is more dear to them than their own suffering—they are afraid that they will lose it—they feel it, like a whip cracking over their heads, striking them and yet befriending them; it wounds them, but it also reassures them.
    Ugo Betti, *Landslide* (1936)

————

WENSLEY CLARKSON was one of Britain's most successful young journalists before leaving London for Los Angeles with his wife and four children in 1991—an experience which inspired his book, *A Year In La La Land*. His other books include the tabloid exposé, *Dog Eat Dog*, as well as numerous best-selling true crime books, including *Hell Hath No Fury* and *Deadly Seduction*. He has written biographies of actors Mel Gibson and Tom Cruise, as well as a highly acclaimed book about movie director Quentin Tarantino. He currently divides his time between homes in London and California. *Slave Girls* is his fourteenth book.